John Townsend

The South Alone, should Govern the South. And African

slavery

Should be Controlled by those only, who are Friendly to it. Third Edition

John Townsend

The South Alone, should Govern the South. And African slavery
Should be Controlled by those only, who are Friendly to it. Third Edition

ISBN/EAN: 9783744728553

Printed in Europe, USA, Canada, Australia, Japan

Cover: Foto ©ninafisch / pixelio.de

More available books at **www.hansebooks.com**

THE

SOUTH ALONE,

SHOULD GOVERN

THE SOUTH.

AND

AFRICAN SLAVERY

SHOULD BE CONTROLLED

BY

THOSE ONLY,

WHO ARE FRIENDLY TO IT.

THIRD EDITION.

☞ Read and send to your Neighbor. ☜

CHARLESTON:

STEAM-POWER PRESSES OF EVANS & COGSWELL.

No. 3 Broad and 103 East Bay Street.

1860.

MEN OF THE SOUTH.

The subject before you, may be disagreeable to contemplate; and the examination of it may be irksome. But it is one, which deeply concerns you.

Time too, is fast hurrying the Question to your hearthstones. It will soon press upon you; and you will not be *allowed* to postpone the Decision.

How then do you decide?

Is it for manly RESISTANCE; to be followed, with security and a prosperous end?

——— or ———

Is it for SUBMISSION; and a short inglorious ease: to be followed with certain ruin?

Say! and after you have made your Decision, write it, upon the door-posts of your habitations, that all who enter may know, what is the fate you have chosen for those whom you cherish within.

CONSTITUTION OF 1860 ASSOCIATION.

I.—The members whose names are hereto subscribed, constitute themselves an Association, for the purpose of promoting resistance, by the slaveholding States, to the aggressions of the non-slaveholding States.

II.—The Association shall have a President, to be selected by a majority of the members present, and a Recording Secretary, to be appointed by the President.

III.—There shall be appointed, by the President, an Executive Committee, to consist of fifteen members, to whom shall be entrusted such duties for promoting the objects of the Association, as shall, in its discretion, be necessary, with power to appoint under it a Committee of Publication, and such other committees as it may deem proper.

IV.—Upon subscribing these articles, each member shall pay the sum of five dollars to the Treasurer, who shall be appointed by the Executive Committee.

V.—The Association shall be convened whenever in the opinion of the President, or of the Executive Committee it shall be deemed requisite.

The Secretary and Treasurer of the 1860 Association, is Mr. Wᴍ Tᴇɴɴᴇɴᴛ, Jʀ., No. 6 Broad Street, Charleston.

MEETING IN ST. JOHN'S COLLETON.

Agreeably to a call for a public meeting of the citizens of St. John's Colleton, to be held at Rockville, to receive the report of their delegates to the Democratic State Convention, lately held in Columbia, a meeting was held for that purpose on Thursday, the 7th inst.

Mr. TOWNSEND then presented the report as one of the delegates; and afterwards an address, in vindication of the 10th resolution of the St. John's Colleton series, recommending the policy of a Southern Confederacy.

After he had concluded, Mr. RICHARD F. JENKINS, one of the alternate delegates who was appointed to the late Convention, offered the following mble and resolution, which was unanimously adopted :

Whereas, the topics discussed in the address of the Hon. JOHN TOWNSEND, which he has just presented to us, being the *condition of the South* in the present Union, and her gloomy *prospects for the future*, together with the *measures of remedy suitable to her case*, are subjects of deep interest to every Southern man, and call for his most profound meditation; therefore be it

Resolved, That Mr. Townsend be requested to have his address published in the public prints.

After presenting the "Report of the Delegates," above alluded to, (but which is here omitted), Mr. TOWNSEND continued to address the meeting as follows :

ADDRESS.

I give it as my deliberate conviction, Mr. Chairman, that the present condition and future prospects of the South, in this Union, are such as to forbid any trifling with her rights; but call for a full and explicit declaration and *acknowledgment* of them. This declaration I have not seen anywhere better done, than in the platform of principles put forth by Alabama and adopted by this Parish when they lately appointed Delegates to the Democratic State Convention in Columbia. Those resolutions cover the whole ground of our rights in the Territories which are the subjects of present dispute; and they do this with a manliness, clearness, precision and force, which leave nothing to be added to them. I think that the prevailing spirit in our Convention came nothing short of the highest pitch of these Alabama resolutions. No platform was adopted by the Convention; because, being invited by the *seceding States* upon a platform of principles already agreed upon, it was deemed courteous to them not to make any alterations in it.

But whilst these resolutions are complete, so far as they go, towards the *declaration* of our rights, no remedy is provided in them (except the *withdrawing* from the National Convention may be called such), in the event those rights are *denied* us. That they will be denied and inevitably lost to us, except we apply some active Measure of Remedy, I think is as certain, as anything future, can be considered as certain. The South, then, cannot too soon, in my judgment, employ her thoughts in considering this remedy. The resolutions lately adopted by this Parish, to which I have just referred, suggest, I think, the only effectual remedy. They are as follows;

RESOLUTIONS ADOPTED AT A MEETING OF CITIZENS OF ST. JOHN'S COLLETON, ASSEMBLED TO APPOINT DELEGATES TO THE DEMOCRATIC STATE CONVENTION IN COLUMBIA:

Resolved, 1. That we heartily approve and endorse the action of the Southern delegates in withdrawing from the recent Democratic Convention, and accept it as an earnest of the Southern patriot's long deferred hope and desideratum—a united South.

2. That the Constitution of the United States is a compact between sovereign and co-equal States, united on the basis of perfect equality of rights and privileges.

3. That the Territories of the United States are common property, in which the States have equal rights, and to which the citizens of every State may rightfully emigrate with their slaves or other property, recognized as such in any of the States of the Union, or by the Constitution of the United States.

4. That the Congress of the United States has no power to abolish slavery in the Territories, or to prohibit its introduction into any of them.

5. That the Territorial Legislatures, created by the legislation of Congress have no power to abolish slavery or to prohibit the introduction of the same, or to impair by unfriendly legislation the security or full enjoyment of the same within the Territories; and such constitutional power certainly does not belong to the people of the Territories in any capacity, before, in the exercise of a lawful authority, they form a Constitution preparatory to admission as a State into the Union; and their action in the exercise of such lawful authority, certainly, cannot operate or take effect before their actual admission as a State into the Union.

6. That the principles enunciated by Chief Justice Taney, in his opinion in the *Dred Scott* case, deny to the Territorial Legislatures a power to destroy or impair, by any legislation whatever, the right of property in slaves, and maintain it to be the duty of the Federal Government, in all its departments, to protect the rights of the owner of such property in the Territories; and the principles so declared are hereby asserted to be the rights of the South, and the South should maintain them.

7. That we hold all the foregoing propositions to contain *cardinal principles*, true in themselves, just, proper and necessary for the safety of all that is dear to us.

8. That the enactment of State Legislatures to defeat the faithful execu-

tion of the Fugitive Slave Law are hostile in character, subversive of the Constitution, and revolutionary in their effects.

9. As the opinion of this meeting that the delegates to be appointed at Columbia to attend the Convention, to be held at Richmond on the second Monday in June next, should be instructed to cast the vote of South Carolina as a unit, and the majority of said delegation shall determine how the vote of the State shall be given.

10. *Resolved further*, As the opinion of this meeting, that if the constitutional rights of the South, as hereinbefore enunciated, be not fully and distinctly recognized by the Democratic party ; or if the results of the approaching Federal election leave us without reasonable hopes for their maintenance, and thus unprotected and defenceless in the Union—then it will be the duty, as it will be the highest interest of the Southern States, to take their destinies under their own control, and prepare, without delay, to organize for themselves a separate and independent Confederacy.

11. That. as a united South is alone wanting to secure to us "equality in the Union or independence out of it," we think it right and proper that South Carolina should be represented in the Convention to be held in Richmond, to aid, by her counsel and presence, in bringing about "a consummation so devoutly to be wished for."

These resolutions, from the 2d to the 8th, inclusive, are taken from the Alabama platform. A careful examination of them will justify the commendation which I have bestowed upon them, as a clear and precise exposition of our rights.

St. John's Colleton 10th Resolution.

But, Mr. Chairman and fellow-citizens, it is to the subject-matter contained in the 10th resolution of the St. John's Colleton series, to which the attention of the people of the South should now be chiefly directed. It is in these words :

"That if the constitutional rights of the South, as hereinbefore enunciated, be not fully and distinctly recognized by the Democratic party ; or if the results of the approaching Federal elections leave us without reasonable hope for their maintenance, and thus unprotected and defenceless in the Union, then it will be the duty—as it will be the highest interest of the Southern States—to take their destinies under their own control, and prepare, without delay, to organize for themselves a separate and independent Confederacy."

The foregoing resolutions were occupied in announcing the *rights* of the South. The necessity of so formal announcement implies that they had been denied, assailed, and put in danger. This resolution deals in the modes of *redress*. First, by referring the matter to the Democratic party, and obtaining from it a *full recognition* and vindication of those rights *in the Union ;* or, failing in this, by the second mode—that of taking our case in our own hands, and securing to us our rights *out of the Union*.

The proposition is calculated to invoke the profoundest attention of every reflecting mind. It is whether our rights shall be given up, and be lost to us, or whether we shall defend them, and secure them for ourselves and our posterity ; and then it suggests the *modes* by which the latter is to be done.

We assume that no Southern man is such a craven in spirit as to give up his rights without a struggle—*in the Union, if possible*, by the aid and instrumentality of the only organization which has any claims to nationality;

8

or *out of the Union, if necessary*, by secession and revolution. The first inquiry then is, whether the Democratic party, or any other power within the Union, is capable, under present influences, to secure to us our rights; and if it shall appear that this shall fail us, then whether a Southern Confederacy will not be our only resort.

DEMOCRATIC PARTY : DIVIDED.

It is inconceivable, fellow-citizens, how any reflecting man, with all the facts before him, should so far have deluded himself, as to suppose that the Democratic party could be *united, upon any common platform of principles,* which could lead to success in the warfare they are now engaged in, with the Black Republican party for the Presidency. After Judge Douglas had announced his dogma of Squatter Sovereignty, and his principles had been ratified, and adopted so generally, by Northern and Western Democrats, the *seeds of death* were sown in the party, never again to be eradicated. The Northern view on this question was in such direct antagonism, with that entertained by the South, that it would be supposed no witchery of the necromancer could possibly reconcile them. The gulf between the two wings of the party, like that which separated Dives and Lazarus, was so broad and deep, that it would have seemed to be impossible to bring them together, in *united action,* against the common enemy. But, nothing is deemed impossible with the "Party Hack" or the "Office Seeker" by trade; and they seemed to think that even this impassable chasm could be bridged over by resorts to "expediency" and appeals to "party success." Indifferent themselves to *principles,* they appeared to think that all other men are equally so. When, therefore, they assembled in Convention in Charleston, they undertook to *cover up* the difficulty which they could neither remove nor destroy, and to accomplish by ambiguity, fraud and indirection, what was too strong for them openly to grapple with. They accordingly offered a platform which they knew was Janus-faced and deceptive, and must necessarily operate as a swindle.

CONTEMPT FOR THE SOUTH.

I make no comment upon the insult and contempt to the South which this purpose implied—a contempt for *our intelligence,* which could not *perceive* the swindle ; a contempt for our political morality, which would *give up* our *principles* for the success of a party or the spoils of office; and the insult to our *manhood,* which could be driven from its propriety, by *fear of consequences* and the power of numbers. But, by whatever motives prompted, the attempt to impose upon the South such a platform, *failed*—as every intelligent man believed it would fail, who had not lost faith in the South—that she still had spirit enough to assert her rights; and who did not believe, with the contemptuous North, that "she could not be *kicked out of the Union.*" The South had been cheated once already in that platform, and by the ambitious Expounder of it; and she had openly declared her intention not again to be cheated. She was insulted, by *not being believed,* both by her associates in the Northern wing of the Democratic party (at heart Freesoilers,) as well as by some of her own sons, nurtured upon her bosom, but who, alas! had learned also, to *disparage* her !

But there were, on the other hand, many—aye, very many of her sons—who cherished her character with more filial reverence, and who would believe nothing disreputable of her; who, trusting in her wisdom, and never doubting her courage, believed that, in her own way, and in her own good time, she would lay aside her forbearance, and plant herself *resolutely* upon her rights.

Could sons, then, like these, suppose that she would go into a National Convention of Democrats, and, for any cause, and under any temptations, *compromise* her principles or surrender her heritage of rights? I tell you, nay, fellow-citizens! They never would indulge a thought so dishonoring to her, as to suppose that, if *principles* were to be surrendered to unite the Democratic party, the surrender would be on her part!

But if they felt sure that the South would stand firm, they were also persuaded that no concession would come from the Northern wing of the party—arrogant as they are from self-conscious power, and feeling, as they do, that they represent the *majority section* of the Union, which, they are resolved, shall *give law to the South.*

THE NATIONAL DEMOCRATIC PARTY BEING BROKEN UP, INTO TWO HOSTILE WINGS: WHAT IS THE INTEREST, AND DUTY OF THE SOUTH, UNDER THE CIRCUMSTANCES.

Here, now, we perceive in the bosom of the National Democratic Convention *two* parties, with principles radically opposed and irreconcilable, and both resolute in maintaining their ground. How, then, could *union* and concert of action be expected from such jarring elements? I tell you, sir, they were not expected; and the breaking up of that Convention, and its failure to nominate a common candidate for the party, are precisely such results as every well-informed man, who had given thought to the subject, had confidently anticipated. The meeting, then, of that Convention, and its proceedings afterwards, were watched by every earnest friend of the South with intense anxiety, looking for the rupture.

And now, I ask, can any different result be expected for the *future?* There is nothing to justify the expectation—I will not say the *hope.* The causes which led to that rupture, so far from being temporary, are *permanent,* and increasing, day by day, in number and strength. No union, then, on *principles,* may ever again be looked for in any Democratic party.

If, then, the Democratic party (the only organization which may be called national, and is not purely sectional,) may be considered as *broken up,* and the Government is to fall into sectional and hostile hands, I ask—1st, what *interest* has the South in the Democratic party any longer; and, 2d, what is the position which she should take for herself in this aspect of affairs? If her rights *in* the Union are not *fully* secured to her, is it compatible with her dignity to hang on to a party as a sort of dependent "make-weight," swelling its ranks, and putting it into power, and then receive from it, (in the *persons of a few of her needy office-seekers*) a few worthless crumbs as her share of the spoils? Can it be to her interest to continue to be a mere *appendage* to a Government whose treasury she supplies annually with more than forty millions of revenue, to receive back, in return, only twenty millions in disbursements? Can it be to her interest to belong to a nation, in which she is out-numbered and out-voted by those who are her *enemies*—in which her dearest rights are at the mercy of other men who have openly announced their intention to destroy them, and who now begin to contemn us in their hearts because of our *pusillanimity* in not defending ourselves? Every feeling of dignity and self-respect, every impulse of honor, and every motive of self-preservation, forbid it. And may God deliver us from the *apathy* which will end in such ruin and degradation!

WHAT IS THE INTEREST AND DUTY OF THE SOUTH, IN CASE THE GOVERN-
MENT SHALL FALL INTO THE HANDS OF THE BLACK REPUBLICANS.

Regarding it then as hopeless, utterly hopeless, to depend upon any
Party, or combination, *inside* the Union to save us, the resolution then
propounds that question which, sooner or later, we *must* solve, *i. e.*—
what should be the *action* of the South in case the Government shall fall
into the hands of the Black Republicans after the approaching Federal
elections?—and this it proposes to solve, just *now*, and *without delay*, by
recommending "that we take our destinies under our *own control*, and
prepare to protect ourselves under a *friendly* government of *our own*."

And here I expect to be met with the babbling out-cry of the timorous—"Why, this is *disunion!*" and with the stereotyped croakings of the
old fogy "Union-savers"—"Why this is *revolution!*" Even so, fellow-
citizens: it *is* disunion! It *is* revolution! Do not blink it; look it full in
the face. Become familiar with it; for the necessities of our condition
require it. Let us hear no more of the *sophomoric* sentimentality about
"the Union"—"the glorious Union—cemented with the blood of our
fathers, and to be cherished for the memories of the past," &c., &c. Let
us brush away these cobwebs, and look at the subject clearly, like practical and sensible men, who have to deal with a great Reality. Let us
realize to ourselves this *fact*, (calculated, I admit, to sink like a heavy
weight upon our hearts); that *the Union is lost;* that its *spirit* has de-
parted from it; and that for all *beneficent* purposes, for the South, it is not
longer worth caring for! That union which originally bound together
thirteen friendly States, respectful and courteous to each other in all their
intercourse—gentle towards each other's feelings—forbearing towards
each other's private affairs—not officiously intruding, but promoting, like
brethren of one family, the interests, the peace, the honor of each other;
that union has long since ceased to exist, between the North and the
South! It is now the forced and unnatural *herding together* of two *sections*—spiteful to each other—hating each other more and more every
day—with interests opposed—and the stronger section making laws which
operate with merciless severity upon the weaker section!

Is *this* such a union as a prudent and high-spirited man would, for himself, be willing to live under, or to perpetuate to his posterity? And for
the social and political intercourse between the people of these two sections;—look at the treatment of Southern men reclaiming their property
at the North; and the well-founded suspicions, which follow Northern
men, wherever they go in the South, and the punishment which they
often receive whilst practicing among us the fanatical principles which
they bring with them from home. Contemplate the scenes in the halls of
Congress—insult and vituperation:—the vulgar threats of conscious power
on the one side, and scorn and defiance on the other; and almost every
question of legislation decided by a strictly *sectional* vote. Could it be
worse if the representatives of France and England, or of Russia and
Austria, in their worst days, were forced together into one hall, to legislate *together* for the interests of each kingdom—the representatives of *one*
nation having the decided proponderance in making laws for the other?
Could it be worse, if animals of *hostile natures* were forced together, into
one cage, to fight with each other, over their food?

And is this a connection (for I cannot call it a *union*) such as any man
of sense and courage would seriously contend for, as *desirable*, for the two
sections to live under? I answer, for myself, that it is not desirable; and

I give it as my opinion, that "if the question was put, fairly and square-ly, before the PEOPLE of the whole South—with all the disastrous and humiliating consequences of this *unnatural* connection between the two sections fairly presented to them—that there would not be found a lieu-tenant's squad of *Southern-born* men in favor of perpetuating it!"

THE CAUSES OF NON-ACTION, IN THE SOUTH.

And yet it may be asked: "How, then, does it come to pass, that so many of these people seem so *quiet in their submission* to it?" Several reasons may be assigned for this remarkable phenomenon, the chief of which are: 1st, that the conditions are not fulfilled, in having the evils of this connection, and its consequences, *fairly presented* to them; 2d, that, from the insidious nature of many of these evils—that of Federal taxa-tion, for example—they are affected in a manner, indirect and unseen; 3d, from the natural *apathy* belonging to some men, especially among those who, (like the agricultural population of the South), live much alone, and apart from each other; and which encourages a sort of *Micawber* expec-tation, in their troubles, that "something will turn up" to bring them relief; and lastly (but most potent of all), the *delusive hopes* which are held out to them, by those who assume to be their "political leaders," that if they will make such a man President, or keep such a party in power, the people need give themselves no further concern, since the *President* and the *party* will put things straight for them. This is commonly the advice of those "great men" (*so called*) who, being actually in the enjoy-ment, or in hopeful expectation of, the honors and offices of the party or the President, are apt to entertain extravagant notions of what a party and President can do. We need not, then, suppose that these "great men" are wilfully *traitors* to the people, although their advice is followed by all the fatal consequences of selfish treachery. For say, Mr. Chair-man, what can a President or a party do for the security of the South, even if we had their entire sympathy and fullest inclination to take sides with us, when the Northeast, and North, and Northwest of these United States are hopelessly *abolitionized*, and are now working under a "higher law" constitution of their own? What can a President do, albeit person-ally, and politically, entirely acceptable to us; in a government, the most powerful department of which, (the legislative), is thoroughly *sectionalized* and with the party even, of which he is the Representative Chief, taking part against us with our sectional foes?

How unwise, then (for I will not be so irreverent as to say how *foolish* and *absurd*), is it, for the South, to be placing her dependence upon "Pres-idents" and "parties," when she can work out her own deliverance from injustice and wrong by the strength of her own right arm, directed by her own brave heart! .

Assent to these conclusions would, I think, be the general sentiment of the unbiassed and *instructed* mind of the whole South; and this sentiment would soon ripen into manly and resolute ACTION, were it not for the fatal counsels to procrastination from their political advisers, aided by the womanly fears of "Disunion," and the croakings of political hacks about "Revolution."

DISUNION INEVITABLE.

But, Mr. Chairman, not all these croakings, nor lamb-like bleatings, nor counsellings, can prevent it! "Disunion" and "Revolution" must come!—

12

else, under the rule of Abolitionism, and of the bad and vulgar men, who, like the scum, will rise, upon the surface of Northern society, from the boiling cauldron of *universal suffrage*—there will be in store for the South an endurance of insult and sufferings, of ignominy and degradation, which no people have ever submitted to, except those who were *born* slaves! What, sir! can the gentleman, born so by nature, or made so by culture and education, submit to be ruled by some vulgar demagogue like Giddings, or Wilson, or Lovejoy, or Sumner—himself brought into brief authority by pandering to the prejudices of a vulgar *sans culotte?* Can a free people, accustomed to just and sensible laws, with their families and property to protect, and having under keeping so sensitive an institution as that of African slavery, *consent* to have interests so precious to them, tampered with, by the crude experiments of a crazy and impracticable fanaticism?

Example of St. Domingo and the British West Indies.

Fortunately for the South, history has recorded for our warning the fatal consequences of such folly. Contemplate, I beseech you, fellow-citizens, the example of St. Domingo; and then, after the soul has become sickened by the awful tragedies which were there perpetrated, then turn to the British West Indies, and let that example grave deeper upon the heart the solemn lesson, of the "Heavy misfortune of that people whose destinies are under the control and legislation of *another people;* ignorant of their condition, insensible to their wants, without sympathy or pity, and legislating for them after their own crude, and wild, and impracticable theories!"*

What difference would it make to us, whether our lives and fortunes were controlled by Red Republican France, or Black Republican Massachusetts; whether we are to be the victims of the Pharisaical self-righteousness of Old England philanthropy, or the Puritanical self-righteousness of New England philanthropy? France had her Santhonax; England her Clarkson and Buxton; and the North have their Giddings, their Wilson, their Seward, and their Sumner. And, if it be philosophically true, that like causes will produce like effects, what reason have we to suppose that we of the South shall escape the dire effects of abolition frenzy here, when it has produced such terrific consequences everywhere else? When revolutionary France first took the disease of political fanaticism, her theories about the "Rights of Man" were mild and harmless. But many months had not passed away, before the madness had so far got possession of her, that she inscribed upon her banners, "*Liberté, Equalité, Fraternité,*" as applicable, not only to herself, but for all the nations and kingdoms of the earth. The civilized world took alarm at these ravings of the frantic maniac, and closed their gates upon her. But she had some feeble colonies, for which she *had the right to make laws,* and to these she turned, to carry out her theories of liberty and philanthropy! Unhappy St. Domingo! She had not *her destinies in her own keeping;* she was governed by a nation which knew not her condition, and which was under the influence of theories which were entirely inapplicable to her. The experiment was made; she was too weak to resist; scenes of untold misery followed; all that she had of civilization was crushed out of her, and there she stands—a Degraded Thing—a monument of "warning" to all peoples, *to take their government into their own hands, and not to permit themselves to be governed by another and a hostile people!*

* See Appendix, A.

Now, fellow-citizens, is there nothing in this fearful history, and in that of the abolition of slavery in the British West Indies, from which the South may take warning, when applied to the history of abolition in the United States?

Progress of Abolition among the PEOPLE of the United States.

Scarcely thirty years ago, the abolition party was so small and insignificant that it was greeted, even in New England, with derision and ridicule. Now, it has overspread fifteen States of this Union; taken possession of their political power; wields it to its own purposes; has thoroughly *sectionalized* the country; and at the last Presidential election gave to its sectional candidate, although a mere adventurer without any claims to statesmanship, 1,341,812 votes, and that, too, against a man irreproachable in character, and one of the most experienced statesmen in the Confederacy. So much in evidence of its progress *among the people.* And now, let us look at its advance in the *government* of the country.

Progress of Abolition in the GOVERNMENT of the United States.

About the same time, (when they first began to petition for the abolition of slavery in the District of Columbia, and it was objected to by the South as unconstitutional, seeing that Congress had no right to grant such a petition,) they contended for the *mere right of petition*, and to have their petitions *read*. Advancing, step by step, they succeeded in breaking down every rule of Congress which was placed, as a barrier in their way. Anti-slavery petitions have since poured in, like a flood, upon Congress, (the common Legislature of the Confederacy), couched in language the most offensive and insulting to the people and institutions of half the States therein represented:—petitions to abolish slavery in the forts and dock-yards, and every place else, where the United States may hold an acre of jurisdiction, no matter if it be within the heart of a slave-holding State: petitions to abolish the inter-State slave trade, and petitions to abolish the *selling* of slaves, and slavery itself, in the District of Columbia. They have so far attained their ends as to have abolished the *selling of slaves* in the District of Columbia, under penalty, of taking away the negro from his master and *setting him free.* Emboldened by success, they have within the present session of Congress, introduced a resolution demanding the abolition of slavery *wherever it exists;* which, to the surprise of many, has received the support of, I believe, sixty-five of their members of Congress. And the great Representative Head of their party, seeing, as he thinks, that there is irreconcilable hostility between the two forms of labor, peculiar to the two sections; declares that, in that "irrepressible conflict" which is about to take place, *slavery must be abolished;* and, as the North will soon have the power in the Executive and the Judiciary, and as they now have it in the Legislative Departments of the Government, that the *North must do it!"*

The aim of the Black Republican Party—the total abolition of Slavery at the South.

Are these idle words—or are they the well-considered axioms of one who is considered the most sagacious as well as the most influential of the *leaders* who direct the policy of *political* abolitionism? Let no man then delude himself that the Black Republican party will stop short of the *total abolition of slavery in the South, as soon as they get the power and control of the Government into their own hands. Is it the policy of the South to *wait* for that to take place, or to anticipate it by putting herself *beyond the influence of their policy or the operation of their laws?* I answer, in the language of the resolution, that " both her duty and highest interest require she should so act." By what means? The resolution answers : " By *taking their destinies under their own control*, and *preparing, without delay, to organize for themselves a separate and independent confederacy.*"

The resolution, also, takes us out of that class (so abominable in the eyes of Union-sentimentalists and " Union-savers")—who are known as " Disunionists *per se*,"—for it makes this action to depend upon the circumstance, of the result of the "approaching Federal elections, leaving us without reasonable hopes of *maintaining our rights,* and thus unprotected and defenceless in the Union." Can any, the veriest poltroon, object to this? And this leads us to the examination, of what the result of the approaching Federal election is likely to be.

With a Black Republican President, and Congress; to be followed by a Black Republican Judiciary :—what then?

Who is there so brave in hope as to suppose that the Democratic party can carry the Presidential election, even if it be taken into the House of Representatives?—for, in the face of the present divisions among them, I suppose no one will claim a victory in the electoral college. The *Executive* Department of this Government, then, I consider as lost to the South, even if it be of any value to us should we gain it. The approaching Federal elections will also disclose to the South that the *House of Representatives* is also hopelessly lost to us by a largely *increased* Black Republican majority, and our feeble majority in the *Senate* weakened, dispirited, and broken down by all the adverse influences which shall be brought to bear upon them from Black Republican constituencies at home, and a Black Republican Executive in Washington, will be powerless to protect and defend us. What then?

Shall we wait until Mr. Lincoln shall be borne into Washington upon the swelling tide of a triumphant Black Republicanism; with a surging wave of Black Republican Representatives sweeping in after him; and, both together, bearing down everything before them? Shall we put ourselves on our good behaviour, and *wait*, whilst he is organizing his cabinet and distributing his offices; to see, what tide-waitership he will confer on Louisiana and Georgia; what collectorship of customs on Florida and South Carolina; and what little Post-office he will entrust to Alabama and Mississippi and the rest of the Southern culprits who have dared to find fault with the Government? Shall we *wait*, until, as Commander-in-Chief of the Army and Navy of the United States, he takes possession of those engines of power to compel obedience ; and of the Treasury of the Government, to keep them on foot, and to bribe *traitors* amongst ourselves, the more securely to establish his power? Shall we *wait*, and, " with bated breath and whispering humbleness," permit, or aid him, in taxing us to fill his Treasury?—to be used, if need be, to our own subjugation—or, as it is now distributed, to foster the industry of the *abolitionized North,* at the expense of the South?

I answer, without any hesitation on my part, that it is neither the duty nor the interest of the South, to wait in this Union a single day after it shall be ascertained that a Black Republican President has been elected; but that we should proceed forthwith to organize a government for ourselves, and withdraw from the fatal connection.

PEACEABLE SECESSION—OUR RIGHT.

Our right *peaceably* to do this I have never entertained a doubt of; and I think, if it be resolved on by a number of States in *co-operation*, bringing with them sufficient power to organize a proper government, it will not be disputed by our enemies. But if it be, I am ready to *fight for it*, as every people must expect to do when their rights are invaded. Whilst, however, I think that the South should be armed and equipped in every respect, and ready and prepared for any emergency, I do not think that the Black Republican party in this Confederacy have yet become so hardened in the perpetration of wrongs and injustice, and so tenacious yet of the spoils of the Government, as to undertake a *forcible subjugation* of the South to their detestable control. The eight seceding States stand upon principles, in the justice of which, nine other States concur with them. The moral influence of their position, will then be very strong in the domestic family of States of which they were lately members; and *either* terms of reconciliation, satisfactory to all parties will be proposed, and *new guarantees* given to the South for the fullest protection of their rights of person and property, and their unlimited expansion in the Union; or an *amicable separation* will be agreed on, as between sovereign and independent nations—leaving each to pursue their career of prosperity, as may best suit their respective circumstances.

This will be the "Disunion," so dreaded by the timorous; and this, the "Revolution," so growled over by the old fogies. We do not deny, (for we deeply feel them), the grave considerations which should accompany the idea of a dissolution of this Union. We are aware that revolutions are seldom otherwise than perilous and uncertain; and that they should never be undertaken, except with great caution, and from ample cause; with full preparation of means, and after a careful survey of the whole ground. But there are Evils, which, in their actual endurance, and their certain prospects, are so great, and so overwhelming when they do come, as to justify all the hazards which may belong to a revolution. We think the condition of the South, in relation to the Black Republican party of these United States, furnishes such a case.

OUR UNION WAS A UNION OF WHITE MEN, NOT OF WHITE MEN, AND NEGROES, ON AN EQUALITY WITH THEM.

This Union was formed by men of the *white race*, for *white* men and their posterity. It was made to secure to *them* the blessings of peace and the protection of their property—of which *negro slaves* were a well understood and fully recognized species. But this species of property has constantly been warred upon, and the holders of it unceasingly villified and insulted by certain parties in the Union, whose misplaced sympathies for the negro, have made them unmindful of their obligations to their partners of the white race. Wrong, at their hands, has followed wrong in such rapid succession, and provocation and injustice have been heaped upon the South with such increased aggravation, that even the most callous to such things, have lost all hope of saving the Union, and now look upon its dissolution as only a question of time. I hesitate not to say that I think the time has already come.

I intimated, just now, Mr. Chairman, that when any people undertake to break up their political ties and to assume new relations with the rest of the world—in other words, when they have determined on a *revolution*—that it becomes their duty, as wise and prudent men, carefully to survey their whole ground. This is essential—for the purpose, in the first place, of ascertaining, whether the grievances which they suffer are such as, in the eye of reason, are sufficient to justify such a step; 2d, whether the measures proposed for relief are equal to the emergency; and, 3d, whether the consequences of these measures are likely to be such, as to *better* their condition.

These principles bring us to inquire—1st, what are the grievances of which the South complains? 2d, what is the remedy suited to their case? and 3d, what will be the consequences of these measures; three topics, which can only be glanced at on an occasion like this. And now—

GRIEVANCES OF THE SOUTH.

1st. As to our grievances. I have anticipated already much which properly belongs to this topic; but the half has not, and (for want of time) cannot be told. When we look around over the South, and perceive that deep-seated feeling of *discontent* which is brooding over the minds of her whole people; when we see them worried, annoyed, fretted, in their political relations—it is but reasonable to suppose that there is some *Great Cause*, which, like a foul ulcer, is festering within. When we examine more closely, we find that they have been intruded upon, in various ways, by the impertinent self-righteousness of people whose ignorance and presumption are only equalled by their vulgarity. Whilst, if let alone, and not interfered with, the kindliest feelings would grow up between the master and his slaves, we find these feelings interrupted by a *meddlesome intrusion* from abroad; and the master disturbed by suspicions and uncertainty. Whilst he has a right to quiet and peace in his home, with all the gentle charities which belong to the relation of superior and inferior, we find that relation ruthlessly invaded, and the slaveholder, justly indignant because an enemy has stealthily sown tares among his wheat, and he *reaps turbulence* and *discontent* instead of respect and willing obedience. Instead of a feeling of *security* in the possession of his slave property, we find the slaveholder moody and irascible, because of the doubts which an *unfriendly government* has thrown around the certainty of its tenure. Instead of enjoying the just fruits of his labor, he knows that he is robbed by exhausting *Protective Tariffs*, and he feels that he is impoverished, to contribute (but altogether without his consent,) to increase the riches of those who are his enemies. Instead of the *respect and courtesy* befitting among equals occupying a common hall of legislation, the Representatives from the South and their constituents with them, are insulted by coarse and opprobrious epithets, levelled against themselves and their institutions. Instead of that *equality of rights* which belong to them in the common property of the Territories, the citizens of the South are thrust aside from all participation in it, although it was by their own right arms that the rich inheritance was won. Their slaves are *enticed away*, and stolen from them. Their citizens are *murdered* in open day, whilst lawfully reclaiming their property. *The laws for their relief are nullified*, and their citizens are *fined* and *imprisoned* in abolition jails, for attempting to bring back their slaves.

Their *soil is invaded ;* their *slaves are incited to insurrection,** with deadly pikes prepared for their use; and their *citizens shot down* by armed bands of men, driven on by that phrenzy of Abolitionism which pervades and controls the whole North. Irritated unceasingly by the *rude intrusion* of the subject of slavery, on all occasions, and in almost every matter of legislation, without necessity, and in the most offensive manner; *robbed of their share* in the Territorial domain ; *denied their right to their property* in their slaves, and the relation *denounced* as *sinful* and immoral; plundered and impoverished by exhausting tariff laws; governed by that most *odious of despotisms*—the despotism of an IRRESPONSIBLE MAJORITY, composed of vulgar and grasping men ; insulted by the *swaggering insolence of conscious power,* whose fiat has gone forth, "that no more slave States shall be admitted into this Union ;" and that, in the irrepressible conflict between slave and free labor, *slavery must be abolished ;*—and when the South, to protect herself from these evils, declares her purpose to *withdraw* from a Union so odious, and from further connection with a people so hostile,—this undoubted constitutional right *is denied her,* and she is threatened to be overrun with eighteen millions† of men, to force her back into the Union, and bring her into subjection ! When we take this survey of the ground, and realize that it is the condition of the South *in this Union,* I ask, in the name of a God of Justice, what more or greater wrongs are wanting to justify a Revolution ! Does any one say that this must be a picture of the imagination, and that no people can submit to such grievances, and still claim to be free? Does any one (still incredulous) call for the proof and the evidence of these things? I refer them, for proof, to the political history of the day ; and the journals and legislation of Congress for the last forty years : from the day when Missouri was refused admission into the Union, because her Constitution protected her citizens in the possession of slave property; to the late break-up of the National Democratic party in Charleston, because we would not submit to the dogma of Squatter Sovereignty.

Time does not permit me to dwell upon these proofs, nor recount, in detail, the wrongs which have been inflicted upon the South from the time (forty years ago) when the North began to make war upon slavery, in the case of Missouri ; and when she put under condemnation and the *ban* the great institution of the South ; which, as the common government of the country, it was bound to protect. Nor shall I dwell upon the "compromise," so called, which was entered into on that occasion, by which the North, with her usual sharpness at a bargain, appropriated to herself all that immense domain north of 36 degrees 30 minutes; large enough to make ten States; and gave to the South only the barren privilege of allowing Missouri to enter the Union. We shall do no more than merely to refer to the Tariffs, for the protection of Northern industry, which were inflicted with such extreme severity on Southern interests as almost to beggar her people and drive them to desperation. We shall only suggest to your recollections, in passing, the numerous abolition petitions with which Congress was flooded, and the Representatives from the South were constantly annoyed; the Wilmot Proviso, the Homestead Bills, and the difficulty now in hand of Squatter Sovereignty. We now proceed to inquire, in the second place, what is the Remedy for these evils, and whether it be sufficient for the emergency.

The South alone should govern the South.

The measures proposed are *secession and the formation of a new government for ourselves.* I have sufficiently indicated the views I entertain on this subject. We think that the seceding States should nominate their own candidates for President and Vice-President, limiting their choice within the eight seceding States,* and that they should be voted for and supported without any reference to the candidates of any other party. As soon as it is ascertained, in November, that a Black Republican President is elected, a Convention of the seceding States, and such other of the Southern States as may desire to cast lots with us, should immediately be assembled, with the purpose openly declared of forming a constitution and organizing a government. The election of a Southern Congress should then follow; the newly chosen Southern President inaugurated into office, his cabinet formed, and the government put into operation. And by the fourth of March, when Mr. Lincoln takes his seat in the Presidential Chair, the South would have the whole machinery of her government in complete working order to prepare for our defence, or any other emergency.

Is it objected that Virginia and the other border States will not join us in such a measure? It is not expected that they will; nor is it desirable that they should, at *first.* Their sympathies, however, will be all with us, and their influence in the Northern Confederacy will be of more benefit to us for years than their actual union with us. They will form a barrier betwixt us and our enemies, should they attempt hostile aggression; thus allowing us time to get everything ready, and to stand firmly on our feet. A very few years will be sufficient for this—if, indeed, those States can remain so long with the North in so unnatural a connection with Black Republicanism. Sooner or later, they *must* make a choice, and all the chances are in favor of their uniting themselves with their brethren and natural allies of the South. The "Revolution" will then be complete in its *full* dimensions, and the *Southern Confederacy* stand out as one of the independent nations of the earth.

Results of a Southern Confederacy : 1st, upon the Northern Section.

Important results must follow such an event. What are these?—which brings us to inquire, in the third place: What are likely to be the *consequences* of this measure of redress for the grievances of the South, and whether it will *better* her condition. One of the consequences, not the earliest, but yet not very remote, will be that the Northern section will be separated into two or more divisions, which will, *incidentally,* better our condition. The common bond of union now in that section, is the *plunder of the South,* through their legislation in Congress, and afterwards a division of the spoils among themselves, amounting in *various forms* annually to perhaps $105,000,000.† The great mass of the people in that section are entirely innocent of all knowledge of the *source* from which they

---

*This address was delivered on the 7th June; before the Richmond Convention had met: and when it was not anticipated that any other State would secede from the Squatter Sovereignty Convention, at Baltimore, upon the "majority platform," which had been adopted by the eight seceding States at Charleston. If the South can elect a President *at all,* then no man could be more acceptable to us then the distinguished individual nominated:—not on account merely of his intelligence, but because of his manly independence, and his fidelity to the rights of his native South.

†See Appendix, E.

derive these benefits, although it is well known to the makers of their laws. They see this copious stream of treasure flowing in upon them; year by year; they see it lavishly expended among them, and every branch of their industry abundantly remunerated ; and they innocently suppose that it springs up out of the soil, as it were, of their own section ; and that they are indebted to no other people, but *themselves*, for their prosperity. But, when the South shall bank up this stream, and *turn back upon herself* the fertilizing current, leaving parched and dry the hitherto luxuriant fields of Northern labor, there must necessarily spring up there a scramble for *profits* which they have never before felt, since their union with the South. In such a scramble, New England is so sharp, so self-seeking, so dogmatic and pertinacious, that she is not likely to be a very agreeable partner to such co-States as Pennsylvania, New Jersey, Ohio, Illinois and Indiana. They will, therefore, be very apt to vote her a *nuisance* in the concern, and slip away from her, leaving her to peddle her wares wherever she can pick up customers.

RESULTS OF THE SOUTHERN CONFEDERACY, UPON THE SOUTH : 1ST, A GREATER SECURITY TO OUR INSTITUTION OF NEGRO SLAVERY.

The consequences to the *Southern* Confederacy will be those of a prosperity ; financial, commercial and manufacturing, which the South has never before enjoyed ; and an abundant ability to defend herself against any aggressions, no matter from what quarter they may come. And when the South shall have taken our institution of African slavery under *her entire and sovereign control,* and no other people shall consider that *they are responsible* for it,* in any way ; for its alleged sins, and crimes, and disadvantages to them, as *partners* in this present Union, we shall be rid of the impertinent intermeddling with it, with which we are now annoyed ; and the institution will be established upon a basis of permanent security which it has never yet had. There will then be no *motive* nor *necessity* for this "conflict" between the "capital" of the South and the "labor" of the North, with which we are now threatened, and which is considered so "irrepressible" that "slavery must be abolished" in order to save the interests of the Northern section of the present Union. There *will* come a conflict, no doubt, and a fearful one it will be ; but not between the capital of the South and the labor of the North ; but one *within the population of the North itself*—between the *capital of the North* on the one side and the *labor of the North* on the other—backed up, as that labor will be by the irresistible power of *Universal Suffrage.* That fearful, because uncontrollable, power is now kept appeased by those enormous amounts which are yearly transferred from the South, through the National Treasury, to satisfy the cravings of Northern labor. Those amounts now support the magnificent schemes of national improvement; the building and equipment of our navy and army; and many other projects which they have contrived to make *go on there,* and which now give well-paid employment and content to *Northern* labor. But the time must come, when *this* question will have to be decided :—"Whether these magnificent enterprises must be *stopped,* or allowed to languish ; or the *people of the North alone, taxed* for their support." I do not pretend to say how that question will be decided ; but in that decision there must spring up a conflict between Northern *capital* and Northern *labor* with "universal suffrage" at its back, in which according to my judgment, Northern *capital* is not likely

* See Appendix, F.

to protect itself. With labor and capital united in the same hands, the South has no cause to fear any such disastrous conflicts, but both will move on harmoniously and with reciprocal advantage.

POWER OF THE SOUTH TO PROTECT HERSELF: IN MEN, POSITION, AND AGRICULTURAL WEALTH.

What reflecting man can doubt the abundant ability of the South to protect herself, and to attain a power which will cause her to be respected among the foremost nations of the earth.

The *eight seceding States* alone, possess a territory more than *three times* as great as France, more than *six* times as large as Prussia, and nearly *six* times as large as England, Scotland and Ireland put together; whilst the alliance of the other Southern and border States would increase the territorial extent of the Southern Confederacy more than one-third. Can a country like this, occupied by a people who from their childhood have been accustomed to the most manly exercise, and the free use of fire-arms—bold, hardy, restive under unlawful control—and numbering within its borders 1,800,000 men capable of bearing arms, and who, with a few weeks' warning, could be marshalled at every assailable point in bands of 50,000 and 100,000—can, I say, such a country, and so peopled, be overcome by any foreign foe? The idea is simply absurd.

Next: Consider her compactness within her boundaries; her inexhaustible resources in money, and all other materials towards providing the appliances of war; and her capacity, arising from these circumstances, of resisting, or punishing, if necessary, all aggression upon her rights. With agricultural productions the most valuable in the world, and which make them the objects of envy to every manufacturing and commercial people, and her friendship and alliance to be sought after by every civilized nation, she holds in her hands the very best *bonds* which they can give to "keep the peace" with her. It is a mistake, Mr. Chairman, to suppose that England, France, Germany, Russia, and the other commercial and manufacturing nations of Europe, are hostile to our African slavery. Nations (and even our sanctimonious North is not an exception,) are not governed by *sentiment*, much less by *sentimentality*, but by their interest; and these peoples, to whom I have just referred, are too deeply interested in procuring the raw materials, which the South, almost alone,* can supply them with, for their manufactures, to embark in a silly quarrel with us about the *kind* of labor by which these raw materials are acquired. Not only many *millions of their people* are dependent upon these raw materials for employment and for bread; not only *thousands of millions of capital* are also dependent upon them for profits; but it becomes a concern of government, that these raw materials should be supplied; since it promotes contentment to the hungry laborer, and establishes *quiet* and *social order*, which might not otherwise be procured, except by the terrible resort to powder and lead. The South, then, need be under no apprehension of interference with her slave property from these nations; but, on the contrary, may reasonably expect friendly intercourse. Indeed, sir, no alliance would be more natural than one between these nations and our Southern Confederacy. There would be no cause of rivalry and jealousy. We, the agricultural people, would grow the raw material, and they, the manufacturing and commercial people, would work it up and send it to their customers of the world.

*See Appendix, G.

POLICY OF ENGLAND: NOT TO ABOLISH SLAVERY; BUT TO SEPARATE THE SOUTH FROM THE NORTH.

Many might suppose from the past history of fanaticism in Great Britain, and the oratorical displays in Exeter Hall, that she is in deadly hostility to *slavery* everywhere, and would abolish it here, if she could. But this, also, is a mistake. She would, doubtless, desire to abolish slavery, if she supposed that it was to exist as a permanent institution in a *united* States; thus giving to her great Rival in North America, such decided advantages over her, in their struggle for commercial ascendancy.

We should not forget that, within the last forty years, Great Britain has changed her policy, and that burly John Bull, instead of being the *bully* of the world, has adopted the more humane and sensible policy of striving for the mastership in *commerce* and *manufactures*. In this policy she is encountered by the *Northern Section* of the United States—a Rival, which her cheap labor and superabundant capital would not make very formidable, but which, from his connection with the Southern States of the Union, derive such preponderating advantages as to turn the scales of victory against this veteran of Commerce. Her American Rival has the advantages—first, in the raw material at his doors; second, heavy discriminating duties in his favor; third, light taxes; but chiefly in the *gratuitous supply* of a *large amount of money* thrown into his lap, which he has not worked for; which has cost him nothing; but which has been transferred merely by a few paragraphs of printing, called "law," from the associate section of the South, to the section where he carries on the contest.

Now, what would seem to be the very obvious policy of Great Britain, under these circumstances? Why, to *obtain the raw material without depending upon others* for it, and to *cripple her rival;* and thus place herself on equality of advantages with him. Accordingly, we find Great Britain—in pursuance of that enlightened forecast for which she is so distinguished—first, traversing the globe in search of climate and lands where to grow cotton; and, next, setting her agents at work, both at home and at the North, to agitate, and agitate, on the slavery question. Think you that she is governed by *philanthropy* in this—to substitute *freed*-negro labor for *slave*-negro labor in the production of cotton? She has discovered the folly of this; when, in pursuance of the crude theories of her fanatical advisers, she experimented upon the only cotton lands which she owned, and gave up, to negro sloth and the wilderness, all her possessions in the West Indies.* Think you that she seriously wishes to exterminate slavery in the Southern States? By no means. She has discovered, in her experiment in the West Indies, that these tropical productions cannot be obtained except by steady and *continuous* labor, which the *freed*-negro will not give; that, without *compulsory* labor, the raw material for her manufactories cannot be obtained; and if not obtained, that millions of her people might perish from hunger, hundreds of thousands be ruined in their fortunes, and the Government itself shaken to its foundations. Be assured, then, fellow citizens, Great Britain is too deeply interested in slave-grown productions to desire the abolition of slavery. She agitates the exciting subject, by her agents here and at Exeter Hall, *not to abolish slavery, but to break up the Union.* If she can effect this, she strips her Rival of all his fortuitous advantages, and so secures to herself an unbounded ascendancy; and, with this ascendancy in commerce and

---

* See Appendix, II.

manufactures, a career of prosperity for her people which will amply repay her for all her efforts.

Among the consequences, then, which will follow the formation of a Southern Confederacy, I enumerate *jealousy* and *unfriendly rivalry* between the Northern section of this Union and the chief commercial nations of Europe ; and, on the other hand, kindly relations between them and us.

An independent government for the South, indispensible, to the development and enjoyment of her own great wealth.

The consequences, in a pecuniary point of view, will be no less striking. The annual exports of the South, we are told, run up to the enormous amount of over two hundred millions of dollars, which, if representing imports to a like amount, would afford a revenue, at 25 per cent, of fifty millions, which is thirty millions more than is allowed under the present Union, to be expended amongst us; and would equip armies and fleets for our protection, and still leave a large surplus for other objects of public improvement. Under the present system, the South contributes annually to the public *Treasury* forty millions of dollars, and receives back only *twenty* millions; whilst the Northern section pays into the public Treasury only twenty millions, and receives, in disbursements among her people, *forty* millions. Should any one be surprised at the different degrees of prosperity which the two sections exhibit, with these facts before him ? What would be thought of the *fairness* of the contest between two farmers, to prove the superior nature and productiveness of their respective farms, if half the crop of one was forcibly taken away every year, by a third party, and passed over to his competitor? And yet we hear the South disparaged by her enemies, because, in her race for success, she exhibits the signs of weariness and decrepitude, when this cruel injustice is yearly practiced upon her. And, as if to aggravate this injustice, the cause of this decay is attributed to slavery in the South ! Under an *independent Confederacy*, this injustice will be removed, and the South will retain that which is her own. Our institution of slavery too, will then redeem itself, from the unpopularity and odium, which has been cast upon it, by the injustice of those, who have robbed it of its rights.*

Review.

And now, Mr. Chairman, to what conclusion has this examination brought us ? In my judgment, clearly to the following :—

That a Democratic party no longer exist, as a great National conservative element in our country :—that being irreconcilably *divided on principle*, into two opposing Wings, each bitterly hostile to the other, it is neither willing any longer, nor able, to afford relief to the South ; and therefore should be thrown aside as worthless ;—that the Government of the United States, is destined to fall, at the next election, into the hands of the *Black Republicans*,—a party, whose very bond of association, is *hatred* of our Institution of Negro slavery, and an open declaration of purpose to *destroy it* :—that the wrongs of the South, and the hopelessness of any reformation, on the part of our enemies, justify an entire separation from them :—that as a measure of relief, a *Southern Confederacy* offers itself as fully equal to the emergency;—and the consequences of that measure, will be, to give security to ourselves and our property, abounding prosperity at home, and safety and respectability among the nations of the Earth.

---

* See Appendix, I.

Why then do we palter, and waste our hours in speculations about the availability of this man, or that; or the success of this party or that party, whilst our measure of remedy—ample, strong, and efficacious—lies within our reach, and it requires only *manliness* and *resolution* to stretch forth the arm, and grasp it! Surely, whilst engaged in this miserable game of President making, and thereby neglecting our vital interests—the States of the South must appear in the eyes of the Higher Intelligences above, like children, playing with toys in the nursery!

That Virginia, and other border States, should adopt such a measure with great reluctance is very natural. Their case is very peculiar and embarrassing, and disunion must be accompanied with many perplexities to them—but not with more or greater than they now suffer *in* the Union; whilst, I think, it can be demonstrated that their condition in a Southern Confederacy would be far better, safer, and more prosperous than it can *ever again* be in the present Union.

In presenting these views to you, Mr. Chairman and fellow-citizens, I fulfil a duty which every citizen or section of the South owes to each other —that of interchanging opinions and holding earnest counsel together; with a view to arrive at wise and safe conclusions on a subject of more profound importance than any which has occurred in our political history since the Declaration of Independence. Indeed, sir, if my judgment be not greatly misled by my wishes, it seems to me that we are not very far off, from another Declaration of Independence—the independence of the States of the South, from the *Abolitionized* States of the North.

Whilst, however, I express these opinions and wishes, and would rejoice if the whole South could entertain and act them out—I do so in entire deference to the decisions of the Convention of the "Seceding States about to be held at Richmond." I know how essential to our success are *co-operation and united counsels*. With these it is only necessary for the South to *will* her deliverance, and resolutely to set on foot some scheme of measures, in character, similar to that which I have indicated, and a triumphant future, of honor and prosperity will be before her. So thinking, it is but natural that they who earnestly desire these blessings for the South, should endeavor to turn away the attention of her sons from such beggarly vanities as *President making* and *patching up a worthless Democratic party;* and fix their thoughts upon those measures alone, from which they may expect certain and permanent advantage.

CROAKINGS OF THE TIMID AND THE TREACHEROUS.

But, it is said, "the people of the South are opposed to disunion, and will favor no measures which may lead to it." This is just as likely to be a mistake, as to be true; as apathy and reluctance to *begin* a great undertaking may be mistaken for disapprobation, or positive hostility to it. An arduous but necessary work is jointly to be done: but we will do nothing towards it ourselves, because we suppose our neighbors, whom we have not consulted with, might not be willing to aid us! Now, what does common sense, and common practice do in such cases? Why, the parties interested, meet together, discuss each other's plans—reject the bad, adopt the good. Generally, the greatest difficulty is to get the parties together in consultation; and the next is, to convince them that the work is necessary for their safety and prosperity, and therefore ought to be done. From various causes (many of them, perhaps, local) some portions of the South may be more apathetic than others, and be less inclined to *originate action;*

but who supposes, without libelling them, that they are less high-toned in honor, or less sensitive to the appeal of reason and of argument. Let us then, reason with them through the public press. They will soon be reasoning together through their delegates, in a common council, at Richmond. Let us hope, that they will turn away their eyes from the Federal city, and keep their hearts pure, from the polluting temptations of its honors and emoluments, for themselves and their friends. Let us hope, that they will not forget that they have an injured South to redeem; the peace of their homes to look after; the security of their property to provide for; and the cherished safety of their wives, and daughters, and sons to secure, against the fast approaching inroads of Abolitionism; in comparison with which, the miserable intrigues for elevating this, or that mortal man to the Presidency, become so contemptible, as to be a reproach to their reason, and a disgrace to their manhood.

But what means this *discouragement*, thrown upon the effort—proceeding from the unhappy misgivings of some, and the illy-concealed gratification of others, that *"the South will not act with us,"*—addressed to those who urge manly and vigorous measures of redress for our wrongs? Whence does it arise? Is it the *real despondency* of an honest hearted well-wisher of the cause, oppressed by the huge difficulties of the undertaking, as they present themselves to his mind? Or is it the secret exultation of the man having little sympathy with the South, insensible to her wrongs, and who would not lift a finger to redress them, provided the effort would cost him an atom of sacrifice, or would affect, in any degree, his party designs?

You can readily imagine, fellow-citizens, that, with two such drawbacks upon the cause, what a burden has to be carried by those who would achieve the independence of the South. The former are at heart disunionists, from a conviction that the Union has failed, and that a Southern Confederacy is our only resource. But they are vacillating, timid, uncertain in their views; discouraged by difficulties; and whilst they bring little *practical aid* to the cause, and have to be lifted themselves over every molehill in the path, are the first to find fault should any measure fail, or not come up to the full standard of their notions of success. They ardently *desire a Southern Confederacy;* but it must be obtained without difficulties or responsibilities.

The latter class are at heart, in favor of the "*Union, on any terms,*" and never intend to break it up. Whilst they profess that "Disunion is only a question of time, and that the South will have to resort to it, in order to save herself;" that time, with them, is never to come; and their every act shows that they intend to prevent it, if they can. They apologize for the North, and deny or palliate the wrongs which we have suffered from them. If these be so flagrant as not to be denied; and if, under a sudden spasm of patriotism, they join with their fellow-citizens in calling for redress, the most formidable weapons with which they arm themselves for the occasion, and recommend to their neighbors, are "remonstrance" and "resolutions"— *remonstrance* with their "brethren" of the North, not to behave so harshly to their "brethren" of the South; and *resolutions*, which are understood by our enemies to mean—that "if they aggress upon us again, we will remonstrate, and pass resolutions again."

It is from a class of men like these, who are "Unionists *per se*," that the friends of the South may expect to encounter the opposition which, whether from within or without, will be the most embarrassing and dangerous. Too few in numbers to act openly as an organized party; governed secretly by opinions which, if openly avowed and known, would bring them into very ill odor with their fellow-citizens; ashamed to show the federal collar about their neck, with the badge of their master engraved upon it; "Unionists, *per se*"—"Submission to Northern wrongs"—they scatter themselves among the bands of the Southern Resistance men, wearing the same uniform and using the same pass-words, with a view to avoid suspicion, and to conceal their real opinions,

But what do they among these earnest men, who are endeavoring. as well as they may, to deliver their country from Northern wrongs? Wait awhile, and their work will show itself, in the discord and divisions which they will stir up within these bands; and in the distrust they will infuse against the fidelity of their leaders. Their fairest actions will be perverted, and attributed to unworthy motives. "This man," it is insinuated, "wishes to be United States Senator; another aims to be member of Congress; and they are exciting the people, on their Federal wrongs, to attain these ends." It is by such arts as these that the influence of these leading men, in Southern resistance, is weakened or destroyed. Then, as to the measures of remedy proposed : they offer nothing themselves, but oppose everything; but, as a "*friend*," would oppose it. "This measure is too weak; that too strong, and the South will not adopt it with you." Faithful to their Federal master, and to the "Union," their policy is to embarrass, to divide, to prevent progress in the South; watching, in the meantime, to take advantage of every mistake to advance *their* object. If they were to avow themselves what they are—"Unionists, *per se*"—and let it be seen that they wear the Federal collar, their influence would be at once gone; but, acting with the resistance men, as *allies* and *friends* to the Southern cause, they *neutralize* action by arts such as I have described.

I have noticed these two classes of men—the apathetic Disunionist and the active "Unionist, *per se*"—in order that true-hearted men may be aware of what they may expect, and have to provide against, in their efforts to redeem the South.

To be forewarned, is to be forearmed, and will help to prevent discouragement and defeat when the day of trial shall arrive.

———

[This address was delivered on the 7th June, and soon after published in the *Charleston Mercury*. Upon publishing it in pamphlet form the following Notes were added:]

APPENDIX.

A.

The insurrection in St. Domingo, which was stirred up by the Abolitionists of France, was marked by atrocities; like which the history of the world has no parallel. After suffering tortures, beastialities, and cruelties, which none but a Demon could inflict, and an Abolitionist contemplate without horror, the Whites of the Island were exterminated; the few alone excepted, who were so fortunate as to find refuge in the scanty shipping, then happening, to be in the ports. In the British West India colonies they were spared this *extremity* of their calamity, by the presence of a large force of the military sent there by the government, to awe the slaves against committing bloodshed. But the Planters were deprived of their right, to the *compulsory labour* of the Negroes, under the crude and stupid theories of the Abolitionist, that "the negro was like the White man and would give *steady* labour without *compulsion*." The practical experience of the Planters, as to the nature of the Negro race, knew the folly of the theory: and against the ruin which they saw hanging over them, they argued, they remonstrated, they petitioned, nay implored the government, to spare them. But Parliament was then under the influence of the Abolitionists:—a modest race which ever think themselves, *indubitably* right; and in their morals, and religion, esteem themselves, better than all the Saints, from Abraham to St. Paul. In the dogmatism of their arrogant conceit, they spurned alike the warnings of the Planters, and all the teachings which history gives us of the nature, and capabilities of the Negro. Rejecting the *experience* of those, who through long management of the Negro, thoroughly understood his character, and adopting the speculative *theories* of those, who had perhaps never seen a negro, and were profoundly ignorant of the whole subject, Parliament concocted their scheme of *Apprenticeship* and *emancipation;* and in 1833 adopted Lord Stanley's Bill.

History affords few examples of a Law of such vital importance, having been passed, in pursuance of a mere speculative theory; and that too by a parent government upon so large a number of unoffending, but feeble colonies. But the slaves were emancipated, not only against the earnest remonstrances of their owners, but the compensation allowed, was also regulated by a *theory* of the government, and only £19 15s 4¾d (less than $100, and less than a tenth of their real value) was paid to the owners for each slave.

Of course, the *theory*, upon which the whole scheme was based,—(that is, that the negro would work as well after emancipation, as under the *restraints of his former master*) being fallacious and absurd, the Planter could obtain no labour to cultivate his lands, and they became worthless. Estates, which before emancipation, were worth $500,000, within a few years were reduced to a tenth of their value; but most of them became *entirely valueless;* and their owners, reduced to utter poverty and ruin, have abandoned a country, rendered intolerable to them, by the swarms of slothful, filthy, thieving and insolent Africans; who are fast relapsing into their former, natural condition of ignorance, superstition, and barbarism!

Think you, Fellow-citizens, of the South, that these heavy calamities would have fallen upon the People of the West India Colonies, if they had had the power to *make their own laws* and shape their own policy, under a friendly government of their own? Assuredly not. But Parliament was omnipotent over them, in its right to legislate for them; and the government of Great Britain was too powerful to resist, with even the shadow of a hope of success. They therefore bent their necks, and were sacrificed to Abolitionism!

Now there are some points of strong resemblance between those colonies in 1833, and the present condition of the South. Like them, we belong to a Government, which will soon, be hostile to our institutions. Like them, our Government will have the *power* by a strong and *irresponsible* majority (we deny their *right*) to shape their whole legislation, so as grievously to injure, and finally to destroy our Slave property; so long at least as we consent to remain in the Union, and keep ourselves under the operation of their laws. But beyond this, the resemblance ceases. Our Government is *not* omnipotent over us; but merely the Agent of certain sovereign and independent partners, who have agreed to unite together for certain purposes, and have conferred upon that Agent certain defined, specific powers; reserving to themselves all the other powers appertaining to sovereignty. As sovereigns, each of the partners, or States, has a right to construe the compact for himself, and to revoke the powers, when he finds the Agent abusing them, to his injury, or ruin; and whilst he has no right to impose his construction upon the other partners, they have as little right to impose theirs upon him. There being no common umpire agreed upon, to decide between the parties, it is the duty as well as the right of the dissatisfied party *peaceably to withdraw* from the concern.

The South then has the undoubted right quietly and peaceably to withdraw from the Union, when she finds the Agent of that Union, managing the business contrary to the principles she originally agreed to.

There is still less resemblance between these colonies, and the condition of the South, in her power to beat off these aggressions of a hostile Government, and protect herself, harmless, from the effects of iniquitous laws; in the event of that government attempting to use *force.* The power, and resources of the South are ample in all respects, if united in a Government of their own, for all purposes of defence, protection, and perfect security, within, and from without. All that she needs to inaugurate for herself a career of unbounded prosperity, is, to cease those *unhappy bickerings*, which divide and paralyze her strength; and which are stirred up and kept alive by the miserable *office seekers after Federal honors;* who think only of their own advancement, and not of the interests of an outraged South.

B.

It is much to be lamented that the People of the South, are so slow in believing, that the settled purpose of the Black Republican party, is the *entire abolition of Slavery* in the United States, as soon as they shall obtain the power to do so. If this apathy arises from ignorance of the approach of this great calamity, then heavy is the responsibility of those Public Journals, which as the Chroniclers of passing events, have withheld this information from their patrons; and left them unwarned of the hostile principles of a great Party which aims at their destruction.

Wм. Lloyd Garrison, and his wing of the Anti-slavery party, urge "the speedy abolition of slavery"

Wm. Lloyd Garrison, the admitted head and mouth-piece of the Right wing of the Abolition party in this Country, thus declares their purpose towards the South. In an Address delivered by him at the Anti-Slavery celebration at Farmingham, and reported in the *Boston Liberator*, July 20, 1860, he declares:

"Our object is the abolition of Slavery *throughout the land;* and whether, in the prosecution of our object, this party goes up, or the other party goes down, it is nothing to us. We cannot alter our course one hair's breadth, nor accept a compromise of our principles, for the hearty adoption of our principles." —— —— —— —— "I am for *meddling with Slavery everywhere:* ——*attacking it by night and by day,* '*in season and out of season.*' —— (No, it can never be out of season)—in order to *effect its overthrow.*" (Loud applause). —— —— —— —— "Higher yet, will be my cry. Upward and onward. 'No union with slaveholders.' Down with this slaveholding Government. Let 'this covenant with death and agreement with hell,' be annulled. *Let there be a free, independent, Northern republic,* and *the speedy abolition of Slavery,* will inevitably follow. (Loud applause). So I am labouring to dissolve this blood-stained Union, as a work of paramount importance." —— —— "Our mission is to regenerate public opinion."

I am aware, that many of the Black Republicans (but by no means a majority) disavow, from motives of policy, (looking to party success, and the spoils of office), these sentiments of the Garrisonian wing of the Anti-Slavery party, as *extreme*, and going farther than they intend. But when analyzed, the difference between the Garrisonian, and the Black Republican wings of the Great Anti-Slavery Party, is just that, between the advanced Guard of an army which goes ahead as *pioneers*, to remove obstructions, and prepare the way, (or as Garrison expresses it, to "regenerate public opinion;")—and the main body of the army which soon moves forward and occupies the ground, which has thus been prepared for them. The ultimate design of both is the same; only the main body advances more *cautiously* so as to ensure success.

The Black Republican wing,—heretofore more cautious in their avowals of purpose: but now more arrogant, as the South becomes more yielding.

But the *stolid apathy* of the people of the South, so unexpected, after their brave words of threatening and defiance, in their Legislatures, and State Conventions, together with the apparent *pusillanimity* and womanly weakness, which mark their conduct, and the *facile acquiescence* with which when brought to the pinch, they part with their rights, in worthless compromises,—these, have so justly excited the contempt of the Anti-Slavery party, that caution is no longer deemed necessary, and even the Black Republican wing begin now to throw off all disguise. No fears of a *dissolution of the Union*, (a union so valuable to *them*) are now indulged. In the mouth of a miserable Sympathy hunter, smarting under the memory of the Gutta percha which his innate vulgarity brought upon him,—our Institution of Slavery may be befouled as a "Barbarism;"* and the Southern slave-holder insulted by the coarsest language, in the *presence even of his representatives;* and all this, it is now expected, may be done, with impunity. "Aggression after aggression, has been submitted

---

* "Barbarism of Slavery." A speech delivered in the Senate of the U. S. at the last session of Congress.

to; insult upon insult has been given to a whole Section, and not resented: the South *so* loves the Union, that 'she cannot be *kicked out of it ;*' she is so afraid of the North; so afraid of her own slaves, without the protection of the North that she *dare* not break up the Union; she will submit to any indignity; bear any injustice; suffer any wrong; be taxed to any extent for the benefit of the North, for the *privilege* of being united with them."

Such is the Northern sentiment which we have built up there, by our apparent cowardice in grappling with our enemies; and by our miserable vacillation in defence of our rights, whilst occupied in the frivolous pursuit of making this, or that man, President !

It should surprise no one then, that the people of the South should be regarded as a frivolous, and *blustering, but cowardly race;* and that our enemies, acting upon these convictions, should treat us with the contempt and scorn, which were poured out upon us, by the Abolition orators in, and out of Congress, during the last session, and since. We accordingly find that the South, being now regarded as the timid *sheep* in the hands of the shearer, and too spiritless to resist; and that all apprehension of consequences being removed,—the Leaders of the Black Republican party deem caution and concealment of their designs no longer necessary, and have begun to shadow forth less and less obscurely, their ulterior designs. Hear what Mr. Lincoln said, nearly two years ago, in his contest, with Judge Douglas, in Illinois. to obtain the U. S. Senatorship :

Mr. Lincoln, claims that "Slavery must be exterminated from the South."

" I believe this government cannot endure permanently, half slave, and half free. I do not expect the Union to be dissolved; I do not expect the house to fall, but I do expect that it will *cease to be divided.*. It will become all one thing, or all the other. Either the *opponents of slavery will arrest the further spread of it,* and place it where the public mind shall rest in the belief, that it is in the course of *ultimate extinction,* or its advocates will push it forward, until it shall become alike lawful in all the States, old as well as new, North as well as South."

Of these two alternatives, who supposes that Mr. Lincoln expected any to occur, except the one which his party is aiming to bring about : and that one,—the *"extinction of slavery."* Now, this Mr. Lincoln—is boasted of, as being the original Enunciator of the bloody maxim of the "irrepressible conflict;" claims from Mr. Seward, the honor of its paternity; and has received the honor for it, by being the selected Standard bearer of the enemies of our Institution; and has all the chances in his favor, of ruling over us, *provided we will let him.* He is represented, as a man very much of the *"John Brown"* order, in principles and personal appearance;—as "lean, and long, and lank ; and crooked as the specimen rails of his own splitting, and straggling and awkward in his gait;" with "intellect without cultivation ; naturally inclined to *impracticable abstractions ;* and very apt to get straddle of *hobbies* and very apt to keep straddle of them, to the latter end ;"—" whose doctrine is that the people of the North must conspire to *exterminate slavery from the South ;*" who "claims *equality for the negro* with the white race;" and " boldly declares, that the constitution does not affirm the *right of property in slaves:*" and . being " the warm personal friend and political supporter of the notorious Owen Lovejoy, and of the equally notorious Joshua R. Giddings, no men would enjoy, if he be elected, his confidence in a greater degree."

From such a man, with such antecedents, and such counsellors, what has the South a right to expect when he becomes elected, but that like another Caiaphas, " who was high priest that same year," he should carry out his bloody counsels; if it be only to prove his sagacity, by the accomplishment of his predictions. Miserable indeed is the fate of that people, who have for their Ruler, a fool, or a fanatic, who is hostile to them!

In representing the evidence to show, that the ulterior aim of the Black Republicans, is the *total extinction of Slavery.* I confine myself to the declared opinions of the *Representative men* of that party, who guide and control their measures.

MR. SUMNER :—THAT WITH A BLACK REPUBLICAN PRESIDENT IN POWER, " SLAVERY MUST DIE."

Passing by Mr. Seward, for the present, we will now hear what Mr. Sumner, a Massachusetts Senator, declares to be the purpose of the party. On the subject of *negro equality,* he says:

" As well deny arithmetically, that two and two make four, or deny geometrically, that a straight line is the shortest distance between two points, as deny the axiomatic, self-evident, beaming truth, that *all men are equal!*" ——— ——— ——— " In vindicating this principle, the Republican party undertakes a grateful duty, in which they are moved alike by justice to a much *injured race, excluded* from *its protection.*" ——— —— " We shall help to *expel the slave oligarchy from all its seats of national power,* and *drive it back within the States.* This alone is worthy of every effort; for until this is done, nothing else is completely done."

After the South, shall have thus been *deprived of all power,* in the national government to protect herself, he next proceeds to delight his audience, with the *consequences* of that measure, so intensely gratifying to them,——

" *Prostrate the slave oligarchy,* and the national government will be at length *divorced from slavery,* and the national policy be *changed from slavery* to freedom. *Prostrate the slave oligarchy,* and the North will be admitted to its just share in the trusts and honors of the republic. *Prostrate the slave oligarchy,* and a mighty victory of peace will be won, whose influence on the future of our country and of mankind, no imagination can paint. *Prostrated, exposed,* and *permanently expelled* from illgotten power, the oligarchy will soon *cease to exist* as a political combination. Its *final doom* may *be postponed, but it is certain.* Languishing, it may live yet longer, but it *will surely die.* Yes, fellow-citizens, *surely it will die,*—when disappointed in its purposes,— driven back within the States, and constrained within these limits, it can no longer rule the Republic as a plantation of slaves at home; can no longer menace Territories with its five-headed device to compel labor without wages; can no longer fasten upon the constitution an interpretation which makes merchandise of men, and gives a disgraceful immunity to the brokers of human flesh, and the butchers of human hearts; and when it can no longer grind flesh and blood, groans and sighs, the tears of mothers and the cries of children into the cement of a barbarous political power! Surely, then, in its *retreat,* smarting under the indignation of an aroused people, and the concurring judgment of the civilized world *it must die ;*—it *may be, as a poisoned rat dies,* of *rage in its hole.* (Enthusiastic applause.) Meanwhile all good omens are ours. The *work cannot stop.* Quickened by the triumph, *now at hand,*—with a *Republican President* in power, State after State, quitting the condition of a territory, and *spurning slavery,* will be welcomed into our plural unit, and joining hands together, will *become a belt of fire about the slave States, in which slavery must die.*"

The address, in which these purposes of the Black Republican party are thus proclaimed, and which were received with such "enthusiastic applause," as we are told,—was delivered in the great *conservative* city of New York, on the invitation of the " Young Men's Republican Union"; and before an audience so large, that the immense hall of the "Cooper Institute" was crammed, in every part, to its utmost capacity; each individual of whom, had paid 25 cents for the delight of listening to such sentiments! This is noteworthy, as indicating the feelings of our "brethren" at the North, towards us; and what we may expect from them, when they get us completely in their power.

It was to have been expected, that when a creature, so really contemptible, as Charles Sumner,—although "Senator," so called, from Massachusetts, too, under the frivolous, but false pretence of injuries received, ran away from his duties in Washington, and went yelping over Europe like a whipped hound,—was about to deliver a harangue, he would be avoided by people of good taste, from contempt for the *man*.

It might also have been expected, that after he returned home, and had delivered himself of the intensified venom which he had been accumulating for two years, and had distilled to highest proof, in revenge for the *gutta percha;*—that after he had abused the privilege of the Senate and vilified and outraged the South, by one of the most extraordinary harangues which hatred and malignity could compound, or vulgarity belch forth,*— after conduct such as this, it was to be expected, I say, that he would have been *frowned upon*, by every patriotic friend of the Union, who had a proper regard to the courtesies which were due to their co-States of the South. Instead of this, however, we are left to infer, from the enthusiasm with which he was received, that these very insults to the South, and the bitterness of hatred, with which he assailed her people, were the deeds of merit, which recommended him to the favor of his audience. The incense which was offered him, is reported as follows:

" Mr. Sumner appeared on the rostrum precisely at eight o'clock, and was received with an outburst of excited enthusiasm which defies all description. The applause with which he was greeted was unanimous and intense. Cheer after cheer arose, loud and vociferous; men stood up and waved their handkerchiefs and their hats till scarcely anything else could be seen; the ladies clapped their little hands, and shouts of applause were heard from every part of the room. Mr. Sumner all the while stood calmly bowing in response; and it was not until several minutes had elapsed that the commotion ceased."

It would then be a dangerous mistake in the people of the South, to suppose, that these are the sentiments of Charles Sumner alone. On the contrary he is only the Mouth-piece of those men in the Black Republican ranks, who are destined to shape its measures. The very *violence* of his hostility to the South, is just the quality which makes him so popular with his party: and this is in conformity with a principle, to which History bears undivided support,—and that is, that in all Parties founded on passion, instead of reason (like the *abolition*,) *moderate* men soon lose their influence, and the more violent and extreme in their views, take their place, and govern the party. What then can the South expect from such raving fanatics as Sumner, and *his* followers, as Rulers and Masters!

" Long John" Wentworth :—that, if the Union be preserved, under Black Republican Presidents, for a few years,—then, " Emancipation of all the Slaves."

We have heard the savage vauntings of Black Republicanism, from the East, now let us listen to the threats of the ferocious Bully from the North-west. I make extracts from the "Chicago (Illinois) Democrat."

Taking for his text, the bloody proposition of the " Irrepressible Con-

---

* See his Speech entitled, " Barbarism of Slavery."

flict" of "honest old Abe," as he is called ;—(really honest, there is not a doubt, he will be found, (as "old John Brown" was honest) in carrying out his scheme of the "*extinction of slavery*")—the Editor of that paper thus announces the purposes of his party, in relation to the South.

" We might as well make up our minds *to fight the battle now,* as at any other time. *It will have to be fought,* and the longer the evil day is put off, the more bloody will be the contest when it comes. If we do not place *slavery in the process* of *extinction now,* by hemming it in, where it is, and not suffering it to expand, it will *extinguish us,* and *our liberties.*"

(Just "old Abe's" and Mr. Seward's notion. Silly enough, if they really believe in it, but sported by them, most probably, merely as clap-trap). The editor proceeds—

" Let the South threaten dissolution. *Let them secede if they dare,* when Lincoln is elected. They would have a nice time of it indeed. Why, without the *protection of the army and navy to-day,* they could not hold their slaves a twelve-month. Do they forget *their abject terror,* when invaded by John Brown, and a handful of followers. Do they not remember that he *held the whole State of Virginia at bay for days,* and only yielded at last to the *soldiers* of *the General Government.* Dissolve the Union indeed! We would like to see the South get along, with its three millions of slaves, with *no means of preventing a general rising of them,* and a hostile people all along their borders."

This extract claims attention, 1st, for the *utter ignorance* of that party, which it displays, as to the *condition of the South,* and our *ample,* and *overwhelming power to protect ourselves,* and *resist the aggressions* of " hostile people all along our borders ;" and 2nd, for the thorough *contempt* which they appear to feel *for our manhood :*—which however I am constrained to admit they have too much cause to cherish, when I consider the wrongs and insults which they have inflicted upon us, and which we have so *passively* borne.

The Editor next refers to the late Insurrection of Slaves, which the *abolitionists* attempted to stir up in Texas ; and thus palliates, if not justifies it.

" The instigators of the plot are said to have been the white men who were driven from their homes in Texas for their free soil sentiments.

" If so, it only shows that when one wrong is done another will surely follow in its train. The eternal doctrine of compensation will vindicate itself. Wrong begets wrong, as surely as wheat sown in the earth will produce wheat.

" If this be so, what *retribution* must be *yet laid up* for those who for years have oppressed *four millions of their fellow men, robbing them of their wages, tearing from them their wives and children, beating them like beasts of burden, destroying them body and soul?*

" Justice sleeps, but never dies."

But this " sleeping justice,"—of *servile insurrection,* (to be instigated by the arts and falsehoods of northern abolitionists, misleading our Slaves)—may be avoided. How? By the following programme ; which has been so considerately prepared for us, by our " brethren,"—the " friendly " *Thugs* of Black Republicanism.

" If the *union be preserved,* and if the Federal government be administered for a few years by *Republican* Presidents, a *scheme* may be devised, and *carried out,* which will result in the *peaceful,* honorable and equitable EMANCIPATION of ALL the SLAVES.

" The *States must be made* ALL FREE, and if a *Republican* government is intrusted with *the duty* of *making them* FREE, the work will be done without bloodshed, without revolution, without disastrous loss of property. The work will be one of time and patience, but it MUST BE DONE !"

These are the alternatives offered you, Fellow Citizens of the South :— *Servile Insurrection*, to be instigated by Black Republicans : or,—the *emancipation of all your slaves*. Whether of them, do you choose ? You are not offered anything which you claim, and have a right to claim under the Constitution of our country :—protection to our slave property in the Territories ;—the rendition of our fugitive slaves ;—abstaining from meddling with them at home, or elsewhere, with a view to impair their value, or disturb the peace, or safety of their owners ;—and that forbearance, civility, and courtesy, which are due to us, as *equals* under a common government. None of these, are you permitted to have :—but after being "prostrated;" "permanently expelled;" "driven back within the States"; and subdued, and brought under absolute subjection, then the "manacled dastard" will be allowed the privilege, to decide,—Whether the raving abolitionist shall be left to light the fires of insurrection around his dwelling ; or whether avoiding this by the *emancipation of all his Slaves*, he shall be allowed to sink to the level of *equality*, with his former bondsmen,—a degraded, and (because cowardly) a despised beggar !

I ask again Fellow Citizens of the South,—Whether of these do you choose ? The prompt and indignant reply is—"we reject both !"

But, by what course of measures will you avoid, or drive back these threatened dangers ? This is the momentous question, which now presses upon the South for their decision. If decided in the spirit of courage and resolution, which meets the danger more than half way, and with a united front,—their condition will be that of honour, and safety—safe for themselves, and safe and prosperous for their posterity :—But if unhappily, timid, or treacherous, counsels should guide their decision, and they again back down, and pursue the expedient of *temporizing* and compromise, it will be a dark and gloomy history, in which the disastrous consequences shall be written !

WHO IS "LONG JOHN WENTWORTH" ?

But it may be said that I claim too much importance for the opinions of the Journal, and the Editor, from whom we have been quoting. Certainly, this would be so ; if they were the sentiments merely of an individual, and he, one of no position, rather than those of a leading mind, which controls the actions of vast multitudes behind him. What, then, is the "Chicago Democrat," and what of the Editor, who directs its politics ? I find the answer, so aptly prepared for me, in a Journal which is, perhaps, one of the most independent influential, and wide-spread, of any in the United States, that I readily adopt it. It says—

" The '*Chicago Democrat*' is a paper possessing more largely the *confidence* of '*Old Abe.*' than any other newspaper in Illinois.

" The editor of said paper is his Honor John Wentworth, Mayor of Chicago, familiarly called 'Long John,' from his altitude, which is six feet six. or two inches more than that of the original rail splitter himself. A man of such proportions and of the official position of Wentworth, and of his skill, activity, zeal and power as a political editor, cannot be doubted as a man who speaks *by authority*, when he undertakes to proclaim the principle and purposes of his *Presidential candidate* and *the party* supporting him.

" Having thus established the *semi-official* character of the aforesaid leading editorials of our Chicago cotemporary. let us see what they are. Taking the 'irrepressible conflict,' as proclaimed by ' Old Abe' in 1858 as his platform, Mr. Wentworth, in a review of a late editorial of this journal on the subject of disunion, proceeds to show that the 'game of scaring and bullying the North,' is 'but the old game which has been used time and time again, to scare the North into submission to Southern demands and Southern tyranny ;' that, we might as well make up our minds to fight the battle now as at any other time ;' that 'if we do not place slavery in the *process of extinction* by hemming it in where it is, and not suffering it to expand, it will extinguish us and our liberties;' and that against this work of 'hemming them in,' the Southern States will not *dare* the ruinous experiment of *seceding from the Union ;* for that 'the only thing that can prevent a complete and bloody slave insurrection throughout the Southern States is the preservation of the Union.'

"Thus satisfied that the Northern mission of extinguishing slavery in the South may be *safely undertaken,* Mr. Wentworth tells us that 'a *scheme* may be *devised* and *carried out* which will result in the peaceful, honorable and equitable *emancipation of all the slaves ;'* that 'the States must be made all *free ;'* that 'the work will be one of time and patience, but *it must be done.'* We are next assured that it is only their fear of the general government which prevents, at this moment, 'a general insurrection among the slaves in the *border* States;' from which it follows that, with the removal of this fear, there will be an insurrection which will make 'the peaceful *emancipation of all the slaves'* an *easy task.*

"With the outlines of the republican programme for the *abolition of slavery* thus presented by an editor fully *possessing the confidence of Mr. Lincoln,* is it any wonder that the alternative of secession and a Southern confederacy should be agitated in the South ? What means this *peaceable* 'extinguishment of slavery?' We presume it means its *exclusion* from the *Territories,* and its *removal from the District of Columbia, navy yards, dock yards,* &c., by *act of Congress ;* next, the *suppression* of the *inter-State slave trade,* and the *repeal* of the *Fugitive Slave law ;* and next, the *habeas corpus processes* of Lysander Spooner in regard to slaves. In brief, with a *Congress,* an *Executive,* and a *Supreme Court* all of the same model and the same mind, it would not be a difficult matter, under an *abolition interpretation* of the *constitution,* so to *cripple this vital Southern institution* of slavery as soon to render even a faithful Virginia field hand, now worth over a thousand dollars, *utterly worthless* to his master.

"And such, we doubt not, is this *peaceful* republican programme for the conversion of all the States into *free* States. Are not Southern men aware of this ? Do they not know that *within* the Union they have fallen completely under the *overshadowing power* of the North, and that this anti-slavery republican party have *taken possession* of the North ? Is it not patent to all the world that the 'one idea' of this party is *the extirpation of slavery ;* and, to say nothing of the hazards of a servile revolt, is there not something in this item of *two thousand millions of dollars* involved in slave property calculated to *rouse the resistence of Southern men* to the *point of war* against a deliberate moral and *political crusade,* whose object is the *destruction* of this property?

"There may be reason to apprehend, as indicated by Mr. Wentworth, that, with the election of *Lincoln,* the fear being removed from the minds of Southern slaves in regard to the general government, they *may rise in a bloody insurrection* against their masters. Should this terrible calamity occur, or anything in the form of a servile conspiracy, upon the heel of Lincoln's election, unquestionably the next thing will be a general movement in the Southern States towards secession and a Southern confederacy."—N. Y. Herald.

My design in the present Note, being, 1st, to bring together the various evidence which go to prove, that the intention of the Black Republican party stop at nothing short of the *total* abolition of Slavery in the South : and 2d to show the ardent temper, with which they are pressing upon us, this calamity,—Mr. Seward, the Senator from New York, now claims our notice. But as this duty, has already, been so admirably performed ; and in addition to this, as so much cumulative testimony, bearing upon the same point, has been brought together by Mr. Breckinridge, the distinguished Senator from Kentucky, and now selected, for his talents and manly bearing, as the Representative Chief of the Southern Democratic party, for the Presidency,—I gladly avail myself of his work, as already prepared to my hands; and offer it, as something much better than I could furnish. I make my selection from the "N. York Day Book," July 21st, 1860 ; containing the

"Substance of a Speech delivered by Hon. John C. Breckinridge, in the Hall of the House of Representatives at Frankfort, Dec. 21st, 1859."

Testimony of Vice-President Breckinridge

The extract is a long one; but I am persuaded that no Southern man, who is duly impressed with the profound importance to him of the topics discussed, will consider it tedious; but will peruse it, with that high gratification with which I have read it, recently, for the first time. After discussing several topics of a more general nature, Mr. Breckinridge continued as follows:

"Fellow-citizens, I propose now to offer you some reflections on another aspect of public affairs. We have been speaking of questions that concern Kentucky no more than the other States; but we may soon have to meet questions that come nearer *home—fireside, hearthstone* questions. I disclaim the spirit of an alarmist or a demagogue; yet, since I have been acquainted with public affairs, there never was a time when the interests of this Union were in so much peril, or when the feelings of the people were so much *alienated* as at this hour. Certainly, if the aspect of affairs at Washington is in the slightest degree indicative of the feeling elsewhere, this statement is mournfully true.

"The danger springs from the character and purposes of a political organization in this country called the *Republican* party. I do not think that we yet fully realize in Kentucky the aims of this party, what it intends, and the probable *consequences* of *its success* in the United States; nor do I think that the masses of the northern people at all realize the consequences which will be sure to follow any attempt to execute its proclaimed purposes. At first it seemed to limit its aims to the exclusion of slavery from the Territories; but, like all *aggressive* organizations, its course has been continually onward. The rear rank of the Republican army marches up and encamps on the ground occupied by the advanced guard, months before, while the advanced guard has been marching steadily forward.

"We claim only those rights guaranteed to us by the Constitution, which is the bond of the American Union. Among the clearest of them are the right to the return of fugitives from labor, and the right to live in peace with our domestic institutions, after the manner of our fathers; and it is as clear a violation of the Constitution to refuse these rights as if the instrument were torn into fragments. It is the purpose of the Republican party to *abolish slavery in the United States*. I know that many men of worth and ability in its ranks do not propose to press the issue to this conclusion. But *they* cannot *control* the party, and soon they must fall into the ranks and imbibe its spirit or sever their connection with it forever.

"To show the *spirit* and *purpose* of this organization, I present to you a few *proofs* from many thousands of a kindred character.

From Black Republican Platform of 1856: "Slavery—a Relic of Barbarism."

The first is a portion of the Republican platform adopted three years ago, but beyond which they have now far advanced:

"*Resolved*, That with our Republican fathers, we hold it to be the self-evident truth that *all men* are endowed with the inalienable right to life, *liberty*, and the pursuit of happiness, and that the primary object and ulterior design of our federal government were to secure these rights to all persons under its exclusive jurisdiction; that as our Republican fathers, when they had abolished slavery in all our national territory, ordained that no person should be deprived of life, liberty, or property, without due process of law, it becomes our duty to maintain this provision of the Constitution against all attempts to violate it for the purpose of establishing slavery in the Territories of the United States by positive legislation, prohibiting its existence or extension therein.

"A careful scrutiny of this resolution will reveal the fact that the Republican party make the doctrine of *negro equality* a portion of their political creed—and intend to develope this idea whenever the federal government has exclusive jurisdiction—and by a forced construction of the Constitution they claim jurisdiction far *beyond the point we can allow it*. Accordingly as soon as they obtain power they will not only *prohibit slavery* in the *Territories*, but will *abolish it* in the *District of Columbia*, and in the *forts, arsenals* and *dockyards, throughout* the *southern States*—and will put an end to the coastwise and internal trade, which they already announce that no other slave State, in any latitude, shall ever be added to the Union. I give you these facts without comment, and only beg you to be assured that in my opinion they are *far short* of the *ultimate purpose* of the *controlling spirits* of that organization.

"Again, I read from the same platform:

"'*Resolved*, That the Constitution confers upon Congress sovereign power over the Territories of the United States for their government, and that in the exercise of this power it is both the right and the imperative duty of Congress to *prohibit in the Territories* those *two relics of barbarism—polygamy* and *slavery.*'

"Is this the spirit of our revolutionary ancestors? Is this the spirit of the Constitution? Did our forefathers, fresh from the revolution, and all glowing with their sublime efforts in the noblest contest ever waged by man, unite to form a bond of Union which recognized, and in many respects protected, in most of the then existing States, 'a relic of barbarism?' Are fifteen States of the Union, in the opinion of the rest, *defiled by a crime* fit to be classed with *polygamy?* Yet this is the *insult put upon us*, and upon the memory of our ancestors and theirs by the rambling and spurious philanthropists of these later times. If it be a *relic of barbarism*, spreading over half the body politic, can these worthy gentlemen do less in justice to their own consciences than *labor to extirpate it?*

"The party with this platform carried a *large majority* of the *non-slaveholding States* at the last Presidential election.

FROM MR. SEWARD:—THAT IN THE IRREPRESSIBLE CONFLICT WHICH IS TO BE STIMULATED BETWEEN THE NORTH AND SOUTH—THE UNITED STATES MUST BE ENTIRELY a FREE LABOR NATION.

"Nor is this all. I could produce to you the declaration of its representative men in all parts of the Northern States, going infinitely further than anything I have read. To show the ultimate purpose of the Republican party, I quote its policy as shadowed forth by its eminent leader. *Do not weary* of a *few extracts*, for these *utterances* are the *rallying cry of millions of men*. I hold in my hand a speech delivered only last year at Rochester, by Mr. Seward, a Senator from New York, who is to-day the most influential public man in the Union, on whose words millions hang, and by whose directions millions move. That distinguished gentleman uttered the following language:

"'Our country is a theatre which exhibits, in full operation, two *radically different* political systems—the one resting on the basis of servile or slave labor, the other on the basis of voluntary labor of freemen.' * * * *

"'The two systems are at once perceived to be incongruous. But never have permanently existed together in one country, and they *never can*.'
* * * * * * * *

"'Hitherto the systems have existed in different States, but side by side within the American Union. This has happened because the Union is a Confederation of States. But in another aspect the United States constitutes only one nation. Increase of population, which is filling the States out to their very borders, together with a new and extended net-work of railroad and other avenues, and an internal commerce, which daily becomes more intimate. is rapidly bringing the States into a higher and more perfect social unity or consolidation. Thus these antagonistic systems are continually coming into closer contact, and collision ensues.'

"Yes, 'collision ensues,' and his prophecy was fulfilled in less than twelve month after it was made.

"'Shall I tell you what this collision means?' It is an *irrepressible conflict* between opposing and enduring forces, and it means that the United States must, and will, sooner or later, become entirely a slaveholding nation, or *entirely a free labor nation*. Either the cotton and rice fields of South Carolina, and the sugar plantations of Louisiana, will ultimately be tilled by free labor, and Charleston and New Orleans become marts for legitimate merchandise alone, or else the rye fields and wheat fields of Massachusetts and New York must again be surrendered by their farmers to the slave culture and to the production of slaves, and Boston and New

York become once more markets for trade in the bodies and souls of men. It is failure to apprehend this great truth that induces so many unsuccessful attempts final compromise between the slave and free States, and it is the existence of the great fact that renders all such pretended compromises, when made, vain and ephemeral."

"At a later period, in the Senate of the United States, the same Senator uttered the following language: (I well remember the occasion and the language).

"'A free Republican Government like this, notwithstanding all its constitutional checks, cannot long resist and counteract the progress of society.'

"'Free labor has at last apprehended its rights and its destiny, and is organizing itself to *assume the government of the Republic*. It will henceforth meet you boldly and resolutely here (Washington); it will meet you everywhere, in the Territories and *out of them*, wherever you may go to extend slavery. It has driven you back in California and in Kanzas, it will invade you soon in Delaware, Maryland, Virginia, Missouri, and Texas. It will meet you in Arizonia, in Central America, and even in Cuba.'

* * * * * * * * * *

"'You may, indeed, get a start under or near the tropics, and seem safe for a time, but it will be only a short time. Even there you will found States *only for free* labor to maintain and occupy. The interest of the whole race demands the *ultimate emancipation* of *all men*. Whether that consummation shall be allowed to take effect, with needful and wise precautions against sudden change and disaster, or be hurried on by violence, is *all that remains for you to decide*." The *white man* needs this continent to labor upon. His head is clear, his arm is strong, and his necessities are fixed.'

* * * * * * * * * *

"'It is for yourselves, and not for us, to decide how long and through what further *mortifications* and *disasters* the *contest shall be protracted* before *freedom shall enjoy* her already *assured triumph*.

"'You may refuse *to yield it* now, and for a short period, but your refusal will only animate the friends of freedom with the courage and the resolution, and produce the union among them, which alone is necessary on their part to attain the position itself, simultaneously with the *impending overthrow* of the *existing Federal Administration* and the *constitution* of a *new* and *more independent Congress*.'

"Gentlemen, is this the Constitution, this the Union your fathers founded? Remember that these principles are *not peculiar to Mr. Seward:* with some marked exceptions, they are the principles of the Senators and Representatives of that party in Congress—of the body of its press, and of the great mass of the people who compose the organization. Upon what times are we rapidly driving! Could such principles have been sustained at the epoch of the Revolution—at the epoch of the Constitution? Did not the Constitution languish in the Convention, until stipulations were inserted to guard and protect our rights? Were they not put in that instrument by the great and good men who framed it, and ratified by the States for themselves and for posterity? *And are not the citizens of all the States bound to respect our constitutional relations, and give the Southern States peace in this Union?* Was it not formed for the peaceful pursuit of common interests, and for the protection of persons and property? How do you receive the announcement that an irrepressible conflict is raging between the States which *shall result in the emancipation of the southern slaves*, leaving you only the alternative to *surrender at discretion*, or to yield to *violence?* It is idle to shut our eyes to the *issue offered by this party*. It is folly to attempt to turn over a volcano. It is vain to cry peace, peace, when there is no peace.

TESTIMONY FROM HELPER'S "IMPENDING CRISIS"—THE HAND BOOK OF THE BLACK REPUBLICANS.

"As a further proof of the spirit and character of the Republican party, I hold in my hand a book which is of little consequence as the expression of the opinions of its author, but becomes of immense significance, endorsed as it is by the eminent Senator from whose speeches I have read, and by some *sixty-eight Republicans of the House of Representatives, who represent a constituency of seven millions of people*. It is a book called 'The Impending Crisis of the South,' its reputed author being a person named Helper, who professes to be a North Carolinian. As a sample of its contents hear the following :

"'The slaveholding oligarchy say we cannot abolish slavery without infringing on the right of property. Again we tell them, *we do not recognize property in men.*

* * * * * * * * * *

"'For the *services of the blacks* from the 20th of August, 1620, up to the 4th of July, 1869, an interval of precisely two hundred and forty-eight years, ten months and fourteen days, their masters, if unwilling, ought, in our judgment, to be *compelled to grant them their freedom* and to *pay each one* of *them at least sixty dollars in hand.'*

"The sum necessary to carry out this notable scheme, amounting to several hundred millions of dollars, it is proposed to raise by confiscating two crops of southern cotton. The whole book is atrocious and incendiary in the highest degree : yet it has received the written endorsement of the Representatives of seven millions of American citizens, and among them the gentleman who is the candidate of the whole Republican party for Speaker of the House ! It is true that some of his friends say he endorsed it without having read it. But if this be true, I am informed that he has refused, again and again when called on, to disavow these sentiments on the floor of the House ; and yet with this significant silence he continues to receive the unbroken vote of his party.

"The nature of the issue we must finally meet is further shown by the non-action of many States. What can be clearer to an unperverted mind than the *duty of every State to prevent its people from trespassing on the rights and property of the citizens of a sister State ?* The comity of nations would require, this between alien communities, and surely the bonds of our Constitutional brotherhood should not be weaker than the comity of nations. Yet few or none of the Northern States have adopted measures to *prevent the spoliation of our slave property,* and to enter them at most points *to reclaim this description of property* is an unwelcome and *dangerous errand.* Nor is this all. About one-half of the Northern States (all Republican States I think) have passed laws making it *a criminal offence for their citizens to give any assistance* in the rendition of fugitive slaves. This is not the case in regard to any other property ; but they hate slavery, and will trample on so much of the Constitution as *recognizes and guards* it.

"The natural result of all things is alienation, discord, and finally hostile collisions. Gradually *we approach the crisis,* until at last the more advanced disciples begin the 'irrepressible conflict' in a logical way, and 'collisions ensue.' The ignorant and fanatical, throwing off even the forms of social and political duty, *invade with violence a Southern State ;* and, though I am far from asserting that the great mass of the Republican party contemplated the late atrocious proceedings in Virginia, yet I assert, with a profound conviction of its truth, my belief that the horrible tragedy is but the forerunner of a blazing border war, unless the spirit they are fomenting in this land can be arrested by a general outbreak of conservative opinion. The very manner in which their leaders and the organs of public opinion, with the marked exceptions I have referred to, *comment on the act,* is *enough to startle every lover of his country. They regret it,* they *deplore* it, they even condemn it, because it was *against law,* and they stand for the law. These are the *honeyed and qualified phrases* with which they characterize the *most atrocious act of treason, murder* and *rapine combined* that ever *polluted* the *soil of Virginia ;* and then, as if afraid that their rebukes were too severe, they immediately proceed to *eulogize the man* and *his motives.*

"The proofs might be accumulated to the bulk of a volume, but I forbear. You need not be told that I have not presented them in a spirit of disloyalty to the Constitution and the Union. I love both as devotedly as any man who hears me. But the time has come for the true friends of the Union to *look impending dangers in the face,* and *he best serves his country* who *honestly proclaims the perils that menace it.* And, now, under the responsibilities that surround me, and by the warrant of the proofs I have presented, and of many others which are easily accessible, I charge that the present and *ulterior purposes* of the Republican party are :

THE PRESENT AND ULTERIOR PURPOSES OF THE BLACK REPUBLICAN PARTY—THE OVERTHROW OF SLAVERY, AND THE UTTER RUIN OF THE SOUTH.

"To introduce the doctrine of *negro equality* into American politics, and to make it the ground of positive legislation hostile to the Southern States;

"To *exclude the slave property* of the South from all Territory now in the Union, or which may hereafter be acquired;

"To *prevent the admission,* in any latitude, of another slaveholding State;

"To *repeal the Fugitive Slave Law,* and practically refuse to obey the Constitution on that subject;

"To refuse to prevent or punish, by State action, the *spoliation of slave property:* but, on the contrary, to make it a *criminal offence* in their citizens to *obey the laws of* the Union, in so far as they protect property in African slaves;

"To *abolish slavery* in the *District of Columbia;*

"To *abolish it* in the *forts, arsenals, dock yards,* and *other places in the South,* where Congress has exclusive jurisdiction.

"To *abolish* the *internal* and *coastwise trade.*

"To limit, *harrass,* and *frown upon* the *institution* in *every mode of political action,* and by every form of public opinion.

"And, finally, by the Executive, by Congress, by the postal service, the press, and all other accessible modes, to *agitate without ceasing,* until the Southern States, without sympathy or brotherhood in the Union, worn down by the unequal struggle, *shall be compelled to surrender ignominiously,* and *emancipate their slaves.*

"Hence, I repeat that the spirit and purposes of the party are *utterly at war with the Constitution* and the great objects for which it was formed. If that instrument is allowed to remain permanently violated in any of its vital provisions, what hope have we for our institutions and liberties? Broken in one important part, it must soon fall to pieces. The triumph of the principles would *subvert southern society, and desolate one of the fairest regions of America;* while, in the end, it would be equally disastrous to all parts of the Union.—The Republican masses do not realize the actual condition of things, nor the convulsions that may ensue. Perhaps even the leaders do not, for they *laugh derisively at our remonstrances.* And yet these aggressions cannot be countenanced. *Resistance in some form is inevitable.*"

"Some members of the Confederacy may contemplate it in the form of a separate political organization. Kentucky, while a single ray of hope penetrates the thick darkness, will resist under the Constitution and within the Union. *Resistance, I repeat, is certain.* Oh, that the millions of our northern brethren could know this truth, and know also that it springs. not from an insulting or arrogant spirit, but from the *simple instinct of self-defence.* It is idle to suppose that we *will surrender our interests without a struggle from the apprehension of failure.* Those who think so have read history to little purpose. There is no example in any age of a *spirited people who have been deterred from defending their vital rights upon such ignoble grounds.* I remember, when a boy, reading the oration of Demosthenes for the crown, on an occasion when his accuser, going behind the forms of the proceedings. arraigned him as the author of the public misfortunes. because he had aroused the Greeks to a last struggle for their country against Philip of Macedon. The result had been fatal to Athens. He defended himself by the memories of those who had died at Platea, at Marathon. at Salamis. and of all their heroes who reposed in the public monuments. He stirred their souls by recitation of Grecian glories, and then—'What though we failed, we did our duty; we acted to the spirit and character of our ancestors. The result is such as God gives to each.' Reanimated by an appeal so noble and so true, the dead body of Athenian liberty for an instant sprang upon its feet, and although the man accused was the enemy of their master, Alexander, those degenerate Greeks, touched with some portion of their ancestral courage, rose out of the depths of their national abasement, and crowned the world's great orator as a public benefactor.

"We cannot delude ourselves with the thought that the dangers that menace us are *afar off,* nor should others delude themselves with the thought that there will be no resistance. Constitutional resistance we contemplate to the latest moment, even against unconstitutional attacks. But when the subject of contest reaches the homes and firesides of a people, who is wise enough to predict or control the progress of events?

" I have seen the growing evidences for the last few years, culminating recently into *proof* of the determination of the Republicans *to take possession*, if possible *of the government, for the purposes I have described.* And I have seen in the Representatives of the lower southern States a most resolute and *determined spirit of resistance.* In the meantime I perceive a sensible loss of that spirit of brotherhood—that feeling of love for a common country—that favor of loyalty—which are at last the surest cement of the Union; so that in the present unhappy state of affairs, I was almost tempted to exclaim that we are *dissolving week by week* and *month by month.* The threads are gradually fretting themselves asunder; and a stranger visiting Washington might imagine that the *Executive of the United States was the President of two hostile republics.* Our wisest and best men observe this growing feeling of *alienation,* and it has become with them the subject of anxious thought and conversation. They are alarmed; it is not craven terror, it is the noble fear that patriots feel for an imperilled country.

" Perhaps the most imminent danger springs from the possible action of certain members of the confederacy. The representatives from South Carolina, Georgia, Alabama, and Mississippi, not to mention other Southern States, say that they represent their constituents—nay, that they scarcely go so far as their constituents—and most of them declare that they are ready at any moment for *a separate organization.* Some of the Southern Legislatures have passed resolves of this character—and we may safely assume that it is the true feeling of the people. God forbid that such an event should occur! God forbid that the step shall ever be taken! We have other, and I hope adequate remedies. But do you not perceive that in such an event the difficulties that surround us would be fearfully augmented? Do you not remember when South Carolina in 1832, arrayed herself against the General Government upon a question of policy connected with the collection of taxes, the issue shook the Union to its centre? What were the circumstances of that day? Andrew Jackson was President of the United States, and he was a native of South Carolina; the question at issue was not nearly so vital as those that now convulse the country; few of the other States sympathised with the movement of that little State; Henry Clay was alive, and with Calhoun and Webster, and other very eminent statesmen, laboured to restore tranquility—and yet the issue then made imperilled the Union of the States in the judgment of the wisest and best men. How much more alarming is the aspect of affairs to-day—*wide-spread disaffection through the South*—an *unrelenting feeling,* growing daily stronger in the North. Clay, Calhoun, and Webster dead, and none, alas! to fill their places. Now is it not clear to the dullest comprehension, with the *government* in the *possession* of a *hostile* and *aggressive majority,* if several of the Southern States take steps towards separation, the whole system would be involved in the utmost peril? Speculate as we may, such is the nature of our system that it is in the power of two or three States to put a stop to the harmonious and regular action of the Government. I will not enlarge on the difficulties which would then surround us. They occur to, and appal every thoughtful mind. When the sad day comes, in which that step shall be taken, no earthly vision will be wise and keen enough to look through the darkness, and discern a port of safety.

" These are some of the facts it becomes the people of Kentucky to observe and ponder well. I have thus, fellow citizens, in simple and temperate language, purposely avoided ornaments of rhetoric and epithets of passion, attempted to expose the character and purpose of the Republican party, and have alluded to the immediate dangers that threaten the country. *A political party expects soon to take possession of the Government, whose animating principle is hostility to the institutions of fifteen States.* What it *intends to do,* I have tried to show: that it will be *resisted,* is as certain as that a *brave people never submitted* to have a great federal bond *insultingly broken* and *their essential rights taken from them without a struggle.* The power of two or three States, indeed *of one State, to precipitate the issue,* invest the subject with great danger. We stand, not in the presence of spectres and shadows, but of *great and terrible realities.* I see on one side, an *unrelenting purpose of aggression,* and on the other a *dauntless determination to resist.*

41

WILL THE SOUTH SURRENDER TO ENEMIES SO DEADLY: OR WHAT?

Mr. Breckinridge in thus giving *warning* to his Constituents of those dangers which are steadily and rapidly advancing upon them, and threatening their ruin; has performed the duty of a faithful Watchman over their interests; and has entitled himself to the gratitude of the whole South. It is much to be regretted, that his example has not been more generally followed, on their return home, by all the Representatives from the threatened region.

And now, Fellow Citizens of the South, with this array of facts before you;—facts, which to every one, (except to the mind which is steeped in sloth, and in a mere animal insensibility,) must carry the unwavering conviction,—That the *settled purpose* of the North is to emancipate our slaves, and spread ruin over our fair country. What do you intend to do? What should be *our* course of measures, to meet, or counteract their designs? *Forcible emancipation*, (they call it "peaceable," "equitable," but nothing can be peaceable, or equitable, which does not meet our willing consent)—forcible emancipation is *certain*, if we remain in the union, under the control of a hostile people, to make laws for us, and to shape the policy of the Government. To be safe, and prosperous, we must be *ruled by ourselves*, or our *friends* and not by aliens, or our *enemies*. It is recorded among the heavy calamities of the children of Israel, that "they that *hated* them, ruled over them;"—that "their enemies also *oppressed* them and they were brought into *subjection under their hands.*" Our subjection must come only from a sensual and inglorious sloth, if they who hate us, rule over us; for we have the right to throw off their rule, and power enough to protect ourselves, and make the act harmless.

The only substitute for this course, (except *abject, downright, slavish submission*, to those who *hate* us), is, the recommendation that "the Republican party must be overthrown." How? By what means? Not, I presume, by invasion and *physical power*. Because, although we have ample power to protect ourselves, and beat them back if they invade us, they have greater power to do the same to us.

Not at the *ballot box*, I presume; because, there, they cannot be reached by us; and if it were otherwise, they vastly outnumber, and can overwhelmingly out-vote us.

Not by "moral suasion," I presume;—by argument, by reason, and appeals to their generosity, and justice;—by none of these;—because, they have all been tried and failed;—failed like the soft influences addressed to the deaf adder,—failed although "charming never so wisely." But when, in the history of *human*, (not angelic) nature, was it ever known, that the avaricious and needy man, voluntarily, gave up his power legally to plunder and enrich himself:—when, that the ambitious politician, *generously*, relinquished his power to rule: or when was it ever heard of, that the crazy fanatic or "one-idea" man, was ever *reasoned* out of his hobby, whether harmless or dangerous! How then is "the Republican party to be overthrown," compounded as it is of classes of men like these? It is simply an *impracticability*, which can never be accomplished: and amounts, when analyzed, merely to a *hope*, and that a most delusive one. It is the retreat which the mind takes, from a disagreeable and embarrassing subject; which it is loth to strip bare, and contemplate in all its rough and knotty, and sharp outlines.

Every expectation then, of safety to the South and our institutions, based upon a *Reform*, which is to take place in the Black Republican party, either originating within itself, or to be communicated from without, will prove to be utterly fallacious, and delusive ; and must operate, (by inducing *passiveness*, and the encouragement of *delusive hopes*) most disastrously upon the South. Let us not look, for our welfare, to those who hate and despise us ; and who despise and contemn us, only the more, because we *look to them*, and depend upon their *forbearance :* But let us look, for our welfare, to those who wish us well,—to OURSELVES alone : and then we shall be sure of a *friendly* care for our interests.

Cease, then, MEN of the South, to turn your eyes in meek supplication, or hoping submission, to such people, as Seward, and Sumner, and Lincoln, and the sullen gangs of fanatics which surround them. Turn your backs upon the North and all its delusive hopes : and with your faces to the friendly South, blow the trumpet of defiance, to our enemies, and rally our waiting hosts, in defence of our rights. Heed not the word " DANGER," so apt to be cautiously whispered by *pantalooned* old women.

" 'Tis dangerous to take a cold, to sleep, to drink. But I tell you my lord fool ——————————————out of this *Nettle* DANGER we pluck this *flower* SAFETY," and so the united South will prove, when, in a Southern Confederacy, they shall place themselves and their slaves under the protection of a friendly government ;—*greater* safety than they have ever enjoyed, from the *nothernmost border*, where the Slave now yields his services, to the southernmost limit, where he is now, or hereafter may be held. And this result, will be *ensured*, by a scheme of measures, which will be devised, and set on foot, by a Government, which is resolved to *protect*, and not destroy the Institution.

C.

The insurrection which broke out lately in a part of Texas, was concocted it seems by Northern Abolitionists, whom a too confiding people had allowed to get admission among them, and prowl among their slaves. It seems that their plan was to fire the little towns, in different, and distant places, at the same time ; destroy as much property as they could ; murder the white inhabitants ; and then after securing as much plunder, as they could carry, " fight their way," as it is expressed, but more properly *run* their way to Mexico. It does not appear that they contemplated at all, keeping possession of the country.

Now, how utterly *Satanic*, does such a scheme appear to a humane and well regulated mind ? And who but an insane, man demoralized by the principles of Abolitionism, could concoct, or carry it out, except with the liveliest horror. Contemplate it for a moment, in the every day aspect of *Plantation life.* Here, is a quiet and peaceful community, with the kindliest relations existing between the Masters and their slaves,—frequent good offices passing between them ; and gentleness and friendliness marking their intercourse ; the inferior cared for, in sickness, and in health, his wants all supplied, and his comforts provided for ;—a gentle condescension descending from the Superior ; met by deference, respect, and oftentimes a sincere affection, proceeding from the inferior ; and a generous confidence interchanged between both. Amidst this peaceful scene, the sneaking Abolitionist appears,—his sentiments unknown, and his purposes concealed. Perhaps he presents himself openly to the master and partakes his hospitality ; and from amidst his own household, begins to practice his diabolical arts of treachery, and bloodshed. Perhaps he selects some retired place of concealment ; finds out the vicious, and dis-

contented, (for such there are among the Slaves, as among the low and c
rupt of every color and country) whose crimes have been punished, an,
who resent this with sullenness. To such he addresses his arts, in darkness and in secrecy : he palliates their faults ; magnifies their grievances ;
foments their discontent : and encourages revenge against his master.
Then follow the Temptations :—the hopes and profits of success ; assistance from the Abolitionists (who are represented as near at hand,) to
murder the Whites ; to rob, destroy, and plunder their property ; and
when all this has been done an easy and certain *escape*, to some friendly
territory, near at hand ; where he will be *free*, and never more work ; and
living the life of the wealthy gentleman, do nothing but eat, drink and
sleep ! With such alluring, but delusive temptations, artfully applied by
an unprincipled man, to the poor, ignorant, and degraded Slave,—(degraded and demoralized by his vices)—is it surprising, that a few of them,
are occasionally enticed away to their ruin, by the artful falsehoods of the
Abolitionist ? And is it surprising that the Planter, knowing the imbecil-
ity and viciousness of some of the race, and the mischief of allowing
them to be *tampered with*, should resent with the fiercest indignation, this
officious, this insulting, this most unwarrantable intermeddling with his
peace and his rights ? Whilst leaving his own home, and intruding himself, with such fiendish purposes, upon the peaceful homes of other men,
what does the insane and malignant Wretch deserve but to be shot down
like any wolf, or wild cat, which is found prowling around the quiet sheep
fold ! And the deplorable consequences to the poor, ignorant slaves too,—
whom they have entrapped by their arts, and enticed away by their falsehoods, from their allegiance to their masters,—what baseness of inhuman-
ity marks their conduct to them ! In the case of the recent insurrection
in Texas, we are informed, that three of the crazy Abolitionists, who
instigated it have been *hanged*, but unhappily they have dragged down
with them, in the same just but melancholy doom, perhaps half a hundred miserable Slaves ; who, but for their meddling, might have lived
happily and peaceably with their masters, to the end of their natural days.

It is worth remembering, that this Texas insurrection seems to have
been conducted, as far as it went, upon a settled programme which the
Abolitionists of the North have prepared for us in all such invasions ;
called "Plan for the abolition of Slavery." As these machinations of
our enemies are but little understood by the people of the South, I think
it well that they should be informed of them. They were exposed to the
public in a

"*Manifesto*, of the New York Democratic Vigilant Association, to their
fellow citizens of the State and country,"
and were published by the "Executive Committee" of that Association,
appointed,—"to collect the details of the history of the affair at Harper's
Ferry, and if it prove that there be any connection between the conspira-
tors, and any political body at the North, that —— sum of money be
appropriated to disseminate the facts, and make known to their Southern
brethren our utter condemnation of the instigators of the movement." In
performing this patriotic duty, the *Executive Committee*, (composed, we
are informed, of " thirty-one men of the city of New York, of vast wealth,
high social position, commanding influence, and indisputable title to be
believed,") put forth an " Address," to the people, from which I shall
make some extracts.

Address of the " Executive Committee of the New York Vigilant Association."

"Fellow Citizens: The community was thrown into consternation on the 17th inst., by the appalling intelligence that a formidable outbreak, *headed by Northern Abolitionists,* had broken out at Harper's Ferry, in Virginia, with the avowed object of arousing the colored population."——
——— ———— ———— "It will appear *that Northern Abolitionsts have long contemplated* a *war of races;* that preparations for it have been slowly and deliberately made; that the recent invasion of the South, was not intended to be an *isolated* one; that its active agents were supplied with *money and arms* from the Kansas Free State fund, and by sympathizers in the North; and that the documents exposing their *Rules of future action,* are founded upon the principles laid down in the speech delivered by the Hon. Wm. H. Seward, at Rochester, on the 25th October, 1858." ——— ——— ——— ——— ——— ——— ——— ———

"It has been discovered that a *Central Association* was organized some time ago, which adopted the following plan for the abolition of slavery. Among its founders were Mr. John Brown, known familiarly as "Ossawatomie" Brown, Mr. H. Kagi, Gerrit Smith and many others, some of whom, as has been revealed, subsequently established subsidiary associations in different towns and cities of the country."

PLAN FOR THE ABOLITION OF SLAVERY.

"When a human being is set upon by a robber, ravisher, murderer, or tyrant of any kind, it is the duty of the bystanders to go to his or her rescue, by force if need be. In general, nothing will excuse men in the non-performance of this duty, except the pressure of higher duties (if such there be,) inability to afford relief, or too great danger to themselves or others.

"This duty being naturally inherent in human relations and necessities, *governments and laws* are of no authority in opposition to it. If they interpose themselves, they must be *trampled under foot* without ceremony as we would trample under foot laws that would forbid us to rescue men from wild beasts, or from burning buildings."

"On this principle, it is the duty of the non-slaveholders of this counry, in their private capacity as individuals—without asking the permission or waiting the movements of the government—to *go to the rescue of the slaves* from the hands of their oppressors.

"This duty is so self-evident and natural a one, that he who pretends to doubt it, should be regarded either as seeking to evade it or as himself a servile and ignorant slave of corrupt institutions or customs.

"Holding these opinions, we propose to act upon them, and we invite all other citizens of the United States to join us in the enterprise. To enable them to judge of its feasibility, we lay before them the following programme of measures, which, we think, ought to be adopted, and would be successful :—

"1. The formation of associations throughout the country, of all persons who are willing to pledge themselves publicly to favor the enterprise, and render assistance and support of any kind to it.

"2. Establishing or sustaining papers to advocate the enterprise.

"3. Refusing to vote for any person for any civil or military office whatever who is not publicly committed to the enterprise.

"4. Raising money and military equipments.

"5. Forming and disciplining such military companies as may volunteer for actual service.

"6. Detaching the non-slaveholders of the South from all alliance wi the slaveholders, and inducing them to co-operate with us, by appeals to their safety, interest, honor, justice and humanity.

"7. Informing the slaves (by *emissaries to be sent among them*, or through the non-slaveholders of the South) *of the plan of emancipation*, that they may be prepared to co-operate at the proper time.

"8. To encourage emigration to the South of persons favoring the movement.

"9. When the preceding preliminaries shall have sufficiently prepared the way, then to land military forces (at numerous points at the same time) in the South, who shall *raise the standard of freedom*, and call to it the slaves and such free persons as may be willing to join it.

"10. If emancipation shall be accomplished only by actual hostilities, then, as all the laws of war, of nature and of justice will require that the *emancipated slaves shall be compensated for their previous wrongs*, we avow it our purpose to make such compensation, so far as the *property of the slaveholders* and their abettors can compensate them, and we avow our intention to make known this determination to the slaves beforehand, with a view to give them courage and self-respect, to nerve them to look boldly into the eyes of their tyrants, and to give them a true idea of the relations of justice existing between themselves and their oppressors.

"11. To remain in the South, *after emancipation*, until we shall have established, or have seen established, such government as will secure the future freedom of the persons emancipated.

"And we anticipate that the public avowal of these measures, and our open and zealous preparation for them, will have the effect, within some reasonable time—we trust within a few years at furthest—to detach the government and the country at large from the interests of the slaveholders, to *destroy the security and value of slave property; to annihilate the commercial credit* of the *slaveholders*, and finally to accomplish the *extinction of slavery*. We hope it may be without blood.

"If it be objected that this scheme proposes *war*, we *confess the fact. It does propose war—private war*, indeed—but nevertheless war, if that should prove necessary; and our answer to the objection is, that in revolutions of this nature it is necessary that private individuals should take the first steps. The tea must be thrown overboard, the Bastile must be torn down, the first gun must be fired by private persons, before a new government can be organized or the old one be forced (for nothing but danger to itself will force it) to adopt the measures which the insurgents have in view.

"If the *American government*, State or national, would *abolish slavery*, we would leave the work in their hands. But as they do not, and apparently will not, we propose *to force them to do it*, or to do it ourselves *in defiance* of them

"If any considerable number of the American people will join us, the work will be an easy and bloodless one; for slavery can live only in quiet, and in the sympathy or subjection of all around it.

"We, the subscribers, residents of the town of ——, in the county of ——, in the State of ——, believing in the principles, and approving generally of the measures set forth in the foregoing 'Plan for the Abolition of Slavery,' and in the accompanying address 'To the non-slaveholders of the South,' hereby unite ourselves in an association, to be called the League of Freedom, in the town of ——, for the purpose of aiding to carry said rian into effect,* and we hereby severally declare it to be our sincere intention to co-operate with each other, and with all other associations within the United States having the same purpose in view, and adopting the same platform of principles and measures."

Together with this general plan of association, the manner in which its members intended to carry out its objects, was drawn up for secret circulation among those from whom it was hoped would lend it assistance in the South. It reads as follows:—

Plan of the Abolitionists : for secret circulation.

"Our plan, then, is—

"1. To *make war* (openly or secretly, as circumstances may dictate) *upon the property of the slaveholders* and their abettors—not for its destruction, if that can be easily avoided, but to convert it to the *use* of the *slaves*. If it cannot be thus converted, then we advise its *destruction*. Teach the slaves to *burn their master's buildings*, to *kill* their *cattle* and *horses*, to conceal or *destroy farming utensils*, to abandon labor in seed time and harvest, and *let crops perish.* · Make slavery *unprofitable* in this way, if it can be done in no other.

"2. To make slaveholders objects of *derision* and *contempt*, by *flogging them* whenever they shall be guilty of flogging their slaves.

"3. To risk no general insurrection until we of the North go to your assistance, or you are sure of success without our aid.

"To cultivate the friendship and confidence of the slaves; to consult with them as to their rights and interests, and the means of promoting them; to show your interest in their welfare, and your readiness to assist them; let them know that they have your sympathy, and it will give them courage, self-respect and ambition, and make men of them—infinitely better men to live by, as neighbors and friends, than the indolent, arrogant, selfish, heartless, domineering robbers and tyrants who now keep both yourselves and the slaves in subjection, and look with contempt upon all who live by honest labor.

"5. To change your political institutions as soon as possible, and, in the meantime, give never a vote to a slaveholder; pay no taxes to their government, if you can either resist or evade them; as witnesses and jurors, give no testimony and no verdicts in support of any slaveholding claims; perform no military, patrol or police service ; mob slaveholding courts, jails and sheriffs; do nothing, in short, for sustaining slavery, but everything you safely can, *publicly and privately, for its overthrow.*"

The document in question continues :—

"We are unwilling to take the responsibility of advising any general insurrection, or any taking of life, until *we, of the North, go down to take part in it*, in such numbers as to insure a certain and easy victory. We, therefore, advise that for the present, operations be confined to the seizure of property, and the *chastisement of individual slaveholders* and their accomplices, and that these things be done only so far as they can be done without too great danger to the actors.

"We especially advise the *flogging of individual slaveholders.* This is a case where the medical principle, that like cures like, will certainly

---

* Does not this suggest to the South the pressing necessity of our having " Leagues of Defence ;" in every community, or *Beat Companies* in the whole South, ready to act at any moment as circumstances may require.

If our enemies combine to invade, and destroy, we should combine also, to defend and promptly punish them.

47

succeed. Give the slaveholders, then, a taste of their own whips,
their lives, but not their backs. The arrogance they have acquired by
use of the lash upon others, will be soon taken out of them, when the sa_
scourge shall be applied to themselves. A band of ten or twenty deter
mined negroes, well armed, having their rendezvous in the forests, coming
out upon the plantations by day or night, seizing individual slaveholders,
stripping them and *flogging them soundly,* in the *presence of their own
slaves,* would soon abolish slavery over a large district.

"These bands could also do a good work by *kidnapping individual slaveholders,* taking them into the forest, and holding them as hostages for the
good behavior of the whites remaining on the plantation ; compelling them
also to execute deeds of emancipation, and *conveyances* of *their property* to
their slaves. These contracts could probably never afterward be success-
fully disavowed on the ground of duress, (especially after *new governments,
favorable to liberty, should be established,*) inasmuch as such contracts would
be nothing more than justice ; and men may rightfully be coerced to do
justice. Such contracts would be intrinsically as valid as the treatise by
which conquered nations make satisfaction for the injustice which caused
the war.

"The more bold and resolute slaves should be encouraged to form
themselves into bands, build forts in the forest, and there collect arms,
stores, horses—everything that will enable them to sustain themselves and
carry on their warfare against the slaveholders.

"Another important measure on the part of the slaves will be to disarm
their masters, so far as that is practicable, by seizing and concealing their
weapons whenever opportunity offers. They should also kill all slave-
hunting dogs, and the owners, too, if that should prove necessary.

"Whenever the slaves on a plantation are not powerful or courageous
enough to resist, they should be encouraged to desert in a body, tempo-
rarily, especially at harvest time, so as to cause the *crops to perish* for
want of hands to gather them.

"Many other ways will suggest themselves to you, and the slaves, by
which the slaveholders can be annoyed and injured, without causing any
general outbreak or shedding of blood."

It must be stated here, in justice to Gerritt Smith, that he has publicly
denied that he was a participant with John Brown, and the others who
devised, and put forth these diabolical "Plans" ; although he admits that
"John Brown was his *beloved friend,* and obtained *loans* and *gifts of money
from him,* whenever applied for."

From this "Manifesto of the New York Democratic Association," the
South may learn that there are at the North a few honorable and intelligent men, still faithful to their obligations to us, under the Constitution :
but that there are on the other hand, very many, constituting the *great
mass of the population,* who devise and would practice upon us the greatest
barbarities, against our lives and property, and the *foulest indignities upon
our persons,* as men. Is it possible that we can continue to live in a political union, with men like these, who entertain feelings of such bitter malignity towards us ?—especially when we know, that it is *through that Union
with us,* that they possess so many more opportunities of carrying out their
schemes of ruin, than they would otherwise have ?

D.

This blood-thirsty, ferocious threat was thrown out at the last session of
Congress by the Hon. Owen Lovejoy, first, I believe, and by several other

ߙack Republican members afterwards, with a view to intimidate the So against seceding from the Union.

It is of a piece with the following fiendish aspirations of Joshua R. C dings, who is, equally with Owen Lovejoy, the warm personal friend Mr. Lincoln ; are now his ardent political supporters, and doubtless wil be his chosen advisers.

"I look forward to the day," said Mr. Giddings, "when there shall be a *servile insurrection* in the South ; when the black man, armed with British bayonets, and led on by British officers, shall assert his freedom, and wage a *war of extermination* against his master; when the *torch of the incendiary shall light up the towns* and cities of the South, and *blot out the last vestige of slavery.* And though I may not mock at their calamity, nor laugh when their fear cometh, yet I will hail it as the dawn of a political millennium."

The conflagration of cities, and an insurrectionary army of slaves, British officered and British armed, would certainly be terrible calamities ; and are just such no doubt, as the Black Republicans have in store for us, when they get us in their power; and Mr. Lincoln, aided by such men as Giddings, Lovejoy, Sumner, &c., shall have the making of laws, for the *hated* South. *Then*, (I mean that fast approaching time, when they shall *have us in their power*, and shall *make laws for us*)—then, they may so shape the policy of the government, as to make every thing work *against* the South. They may keep the armories at the North actively engaged in manufacturing arms, of the most approved kind, and fill their *own* arsenals with these ; and by a system of revenue, skillfully devised, the South may be taxed to the very verge of poverty ; and out of the Treasury which she fills, these arms might be paid for. They might then arm every man of the Black Republican North with these "Sharp's Rifles," or other *improved* arms; and send *none* to the South ; or, (if to preserve appearances), only those which are worthless and cast away. After thus impoverishing the South, so as to disable her from making her own arms, and after disarming her by keeping from her people those which their own money has paid for,—then, may be consummated the fiendish purposes which Mr. Giddings so gloatingly dwells upon, and his party meditates for the South.

But will the South ever permit such a time to come upon her ; when, allowing herself to be fettered by a *hostile* and *irresponsible* Majority, she finds herself taxed to poverty, and without arms to protect herself? I think not. But if she do!—— then, —— —— —— —— —— —— —— she will deserve all these calamities ; with the scorn of all brave and honorable men piled upon them—to add to their bitterness !

But how will the South *not permit* this?

I answer ;—By withdrawing herself from the *control* of this hostile Majority ; and placing herself under the protection of a friendly government of her *own*. This done, and a Southern Confederacy inaugurated, every thing else follows as necessary, and unavoidable sequences. She will have the right to tax herself, in any form, and to any extent, which may seem to herself best : She will have the right to arm herself, "to the teeth," if, she pleases, with the most improved implements of warfare, from the "Colts' revolver," to the mighty "Paixham," or "rifled Armstrong ;" and what is more, she will have an *ample treasury*, out of which to pay for all these, and a thousand other materials for her defence, and progress. "Whence the treasury" it may be asked. As an independent, sovereign, confederacy, the South will have the control of her own *custom houses ;* and with a *duty* of 25 per cent. on her imports of \$200,000,000 she will be able to foot up the snug amount of \$50,000,000 for her *Federal* purposes;

no Northern abolitionists, to spend it, as now, on objects 𝑢ⁿⁱⁿⁱ⁻ to
. Or if she needed a revenue of $75,000,000 as she might do. ꜱᵣⁱ⁻
.g her machinery of separate government, this can be accomplishᵉᵈ. ꜱᵒ⁻
out her people much feeling the burden; since the revenue would bᵉ ᵣ
among themselves (and not as it is now, among a foreign people) and
fertilize, with capital, every pursuit of business.

But this fearful array of *eighteen millions of people*, which Mr. Lincolⁿ ꜱ
friend Lovejoy, and Mr. Lincoln's supporters, Hickman, and others,--
members of the Black Republican Congress of the United States of Nortʰ
America,—threaten to pour down upon the South to overwhelm her! What
of these?—A force like this, of such awful numbers, requires certainly, to
be looked after : and therefore to soothe the nerves, of the anxious "old
women" of the South, (*pantalooned* as well as *petticoated*), we proceed to
reconnoitre this huge, but really mythical host.

It is a very singular, but yet undeniable fact, which is disclosed to us
by the popular Elections of 1858 and 1859, (and which, I am persuaded
will be ratified again, in the Presidential election of 1860, soon to take
place)—that, whilst the Black Republican party have control of a sufficient number of States to give them a decided majority of votes in the
"Electoral college," for president, and to give them a control of the House
of Representatives, (to be followed soon by a control of the Senate, and
Judiciary) that there is nevertheless a large majority of the People of the
United States *opposed* to that Party. At the popular elections in the different States, above alluded to, it is stated, that there were 3,855,646 votes
cast. Of these 1,347,934 were given by the Black Republican party; and
2,467,712 were cast by those who were *opposed* to that party;—making
the heavy majority *against them* of 1,119,778. As a Party then, so greatly outnumbered by those opposed to them, they can do nothing against
the South by *physical* power. The dangerous nature of their power con-
sists in their having a *controlling majority* in the *government* of the country;—in *making* the *laws*, upon which our property, our safety, our lives,
our liberties depend ; and in so *shaping the policy* of the government, according to their crude theories, and their hatred to us, as to turn all the advantages and profits of the Union to themselves, and making it the instrument of robbery, poverty, degradation, and ruin to the South. And all
this, they can do by such artful devices, as not to violate the *forms* of
the constitution.

The condition of the South in such a *connexion* (it would not be a Union)
would then be aptly illustrated by that of some insect, strong in itself, but
which has sillily entangled itself, in the meshes of a spider. With moderate exertions at first, it could easily break through, and free itself from the
danger. But it prefers to be *quiescent* for awhile. Fatal hesitation! Its
artful enemy instantly dashes forth from his hiding place, and fastens a
cord around the wing. The struggle is commenced with much, but not
with all the strength the Insect possesses ; many of the meshes are snap-
ped ; but another indiscreet pause is again indulged in. The enemy again
rushes out, and fastens another cord about another and more important
member. The struggle is renewed ; but now more feebly. Another rush,
and another member is tied fast. The case becomes alarming, and greater
and more prolonged efforts are put forth to break the cords. But alas ! the
case has become desperate ; weakness and fatigue have begun. The enemy perceives this, and is less stealthy and cautious in his attacks. Another,
and another cord is bound about the victim. The struggle becomes weaker, fainter;—whilst the cords are drawn tighter and closer: and now, the
4

last spasm, and the struggle ceases altogether! Every member and joint are now bound fast: and the victim, powerless and in despair, is at the mercy of its enemy! and such mercy!—the mercy which the spider shows to the insect, which he *devours*. The mercy which the abolitionist will show to the Slaveholder when he gets him in his power!

It is not then by any *physical* force which the Black Republican party can now put forth, that the South need indulge any apprehensions; but from the *Laws* which they, will pass, taking away her rights, and inflicting upon us wrongs :—stealthily, cautiously, at first, lest we break through their meshes, and form a government for ourselves; but advancing in boldness, as they find, that by the loss of one right after another we become weaker and weaker; until at length, unable to resist them, we submit to their mercy,—the mercy of the spider to the silly insect.

But it may be asked, how does it happen, that with so large a majority now against them, of the *voters* in the United States, the Black Republican party will have so large and irresistible a majority in the General Government of the Union? It arises from the fact that they have the *control* of the Free Soil States; which are entitled to the largest representations in Congress, as well as in the Electoral College for President. Whilst the united vote of the whole South, with scarcely an exception, amounting, (in round numbers) to 1,128,000 is resolutely against them, together with large *minorities* in the Free Soil States, composed of other political parties —and amounting to 1,292,000, which are also against them,—the mere fact that they have the *majorities* (although some of them very small as yet) in the Free Soil States to which I have alluded, give them the *whole* representation from those States, in Congress. But although this was the state of the popular vote last year, it must be admitted that the minorities in the Free States, against them, are rapidly melting away, and will in a few years be absorbed by that party.

The popular vote of the South is now greater and stronger in relation to that party, than it will ever be again: and we now have greater power to resist them, than we shall ever again have; especially with the aid of such large minorities, now against them, in their own States.

E.

We have adopted here, (on the principle of *abundant caution*, and with a view to place our Estimate beyond dispute, as a point in the argument), the very low figure assumed in the Address,—$105,000 000,

It comprises the following *Items ;*—which show the *profits which the North derive from its connection with the South ;* or, to adopt the more forcible language of the author of the work, "Southern Wealth and Northern Profits,"—the *annual load which Southern industry is required to carry*," whilst united to the North.

Customs per annum, disbursed at the North............$20,000,000
Profits of manufactures...............................20,000,000
Profits to Importers, in Northern cities.... 16,000,000
Profits to *shippers*, on the *exports* of Southern industry,
    and on the imports, in return.......................30,000,000
Profits to agents, brokers, commissions, &c..............5,000,000
Capital drawn from the South to the North 14,000,000
                              ——————————
       Total per annum.......................$105,000,000

I am aware, that, in reducing the amount to this figure, I am very far below the estimate of the intelligent author of the work above named. He estimates these "burdens on the South" at $231,500,000 annually; and I am well persuaded, how presumptuous it is, for any one to differ from an Author who is so well posted up in the facts, and statistics belonging to the subject, as well as in the principles of Political economy, applicable to them.

But, considering the low figure of $105,000,000, as assumed, for the *sake of the argument*, let any one pass it through his mind, and well ponder it. One hundred and five millions for one year;—one thousand and fifty millions, for ten years;—two thousand, one hundred millions ($2,100,000,000) of dollars, for twenty years; and so on, at that rate, for any number of years! The Southern mind stands amazed, and almost incredulous, at these immense amounts; and cannot well realize the fact, until he scrutinizes the *Items;* and then he perceives, by what *indirect, concealed,* and *round-about processes these sums are extorted* from his section of the Union. He can then propound to himself, with the proper emphasis, the question asked in the address,—"Should any be surprised at the different degrees of prosperity, which the two sections (the abolitionized North and the Slave-holding South) exhibit, with these facts before him." What would not two thousand, one hundred millions of dollars ($2,100,-000,000), have accomplished for the South in twenty years, if she had been an Independent Power, to disburse it for her *own* benefit?—*Direct Trade* with its thousand ships, and wealthiest instrumentalities, would have been established; and every city of the South, on the whole line of coast, from Baltimore at the North, to Galveston at the South, would have been flourishing under its enriching influence. *Domestic manufactures* would have occupied every water power, and the whole South,—wealthy, and equipped, and armed at every point,—would have been able to defend herself against the world. And for what does the South barter away these priceless advantages? *Direct trade, domestic manufactures, safety* and *security to her slave institutions?*—Why, for the *privilege* of being united to a people who hate those Institutions,—would destroy her property, and reduce her to beggary and degradation. It would be a singular " Account Current," between the North and the South, if the balance sheet was struck according to the facts. It would read somewhat after this form:

DR.	in account current		CR.
The Slave-holding States,			with the Free Soil States.
Insults in Congress........	00		Paid to the North for
Denunciations everywhere	00		these, $105,000,000 to
Hate and contumely on all occasions... ...	00		$231,000,000, annually.
Southern Slaves excited to insurrection.....	00		
Southern towns burnt down...	00		
Southern houses—ditto and rifled..........	00		
Southern soil invaded, her people killed and property destroyed	00		
Constant efforts to abolish slavery.........	00		

As I cannot possibly form an estimate of the *value* of these items, I leave it to some "conservative *Union-saver*" to fill up the blanks. It would be wise, however, for every *Southern* man to inquire, if such a Humbug Union is worth preserving, to perpetuate annually an account current like this? If the partnership be not broken up, and such accounts soon closed, at the end of twenty years, or perhaps less, there is every probability, from present indications, it will be finally closed by the death, or bankruptcy of one of the partners, with the following *last* items on the balance sheet,—

DR.		CR.
The Southern States in account current with the Free Soil States.		
1850.		1850.
The Slaves emancipated in all the Southern States..	00	Paid by the South, during the last twenty
Four thousand five hundred millions of *slave* property destroyed..................................	00	years for the *privilege* of remaining in the
A like amount of landed,—ditto, ditto...........	00	Union, whilst the
The planters ruined, and reduced to poverty...	00	Black Republicans
Negro equality proclaimed by Congress.........	00	were preparing to
In an insurrection of the negros, one million two hundred and sixty thousand of them *killed* by the Whites..............................	00	*emancipate her Slaves,* from $2,100,000,000 to $4,600,000,000.
Most of the former Slaves in a state of starvation ; having given themselves up to debauchery and idleness............................	00	

Again, I will not attempt to estimate the *value* of the above items ; which the South will have to pay for, at so heavy a cost ; but leave the blanks again to be filled, by the *conservative* " Union Saver," or his co-laborer,—the Abolitionist. Whether, the fearful record just given, shall appear twenty years hence, on the last page of the account Book, between the South and the North ; or whether it shall appear a little sooner, or a little later, no one can predict with anything like certainty. But that that, or some other record of similar import, will be entered up against the South, if she do not soon deliver herself out of the hands of her enemies, and place her slave institutions under a government of her own, which will be *friendly* to them, I regard to be as certain, as anything on earth can be considered certain. The South has but one, of two courses to pursue—*submit* now ; take her ease for a few years ; and meekly prepare herself, for the destiny, which awaits her :—or gathering up her energies, *resist* now; and place her rights within her own citadels of impregnable security.
Which will she choose ?

F.

This notion, on the part of the people of the North, that they are " responsible for slavery," and all that is connected with it, because we are *united* to them under a common government, is at the foundation of all the intermeddling, with which they annoy us. They claim that they are not only justified, but that it is their *duty*, as citizens of the same " Nation," (for such is their view, of what the Constitution converts the partial Union of these independent States into)—to redress all the evils which they suppose to exist, within the boundaries of the whole confederacy. Looking therefore, upon slavery, as they do,—as " a sin," a " curse," a "disgrace," a " barbarism," (and I don't know what else that is vile); and persuading themselves that they are connected with it, in such a way, as to become *participants* in this "sin," "curse," &c., they set up a claim, as of right, to "ameliorate," or abolish it altogether, just according to their notions in regard to it.

This arises from an entire misconception, on their part, of the nature of our Federal compact, and the limited functions of the Federal government. They suppose that the Union, made us *one consolidated nation*, or People ; under one *omnipotent* Government, like the British Parliament. We contend that it only brought together, sovereign and independent communities, under their respective State organization ; that these appointed a *common Agent ;* and delegated to him certain specified, and defined powers, beyond which he could not act ; and reserving to themselves, all the other powers which belong to sovereign nations ; that they still continue separate, and independent, and might become again, perfectly *sovereign* communities, whenever they may withdraw from their Agent the powers which they had previously delegated to him.

Proceeding upon their theory of our government, so false in itself, and so destructive to the independence and sovereignty of the individual States, our enemies claim the right to interfere with the internal affairs of the respective States, and *reform* within them, whatever they may fancy to be wrong. In conformity also with this theory, they deny the right of a State, to *withdraw her citizens* from the operation of hateful laws, by seceding from the Union.

Their Union with Us, claimed by the Abolitionists, as their right to interfere with slavery at the South : sentiments of Lincoln, Garrison, Seward, &c.

Testimony might be piled upon testimony, to prove that the abolitionists at the North found their "right," and their "duty," as they call it, to abolish slavery in the South, on the ground of their being connected with us in the same government, and being bound together in the same Union. It is the staple argument, in all the harangues, of both the Garrisonian, and the Seward and Lincoln schools ; with this very important difference, in the mode of *action*, of the two schools.

Garrison and his school, proclaim their deadly hostility to slavery ; and their fixed determination to *destroy it ;* under the constitution if they may ; but in defiance of the constitution if they can : but finding that the constitution does recognize the right of the slave-holder to his slaves, and does guarantee to him, its protection when threatened with insurrection, and its restoration to him when absconded,—he meets these difficulties in his way, by cutting the knot, which he cannot loose ; by proclaiming to his applauding followers—"No union with slave-holders. Let this covenant (alluding to the constitution), with death, and agreement with hell, be annulled. Let there be a free, independent, Northern Republic"!— leaving a free, independent, Southern Republic, to be also formed.

Now this is at least consistent, and devoid of hypocrisy. If through the constitution and Union they have become connected with slavery, and cannot get rid of it ;—and if by this connection with it, their conscience becomes burdened, as with a great "sin";—the only course they have, as religious, and conscientious men, is to sunder their connexion with it ; and with that dissolution of the Union, their responsibility for it. Such is the mode of action, which the *religious* and *conscientious* abolitionists propose, to themselves in dealing with slavery under the restraints of the constitution

Different is the scheme of the *political* abolitionist, or Black Republican, This hybrid,—(the compound of *Fanatic* and *Political Knave*)—as *fanatic*, has resolved on "the total extinction of slavery;" and as political knave, he professes that he will do it according to the *forms* of the constitution: in the meanwhile holding fast to all the *profits* of the sin, and threatening the South with military *coercion* if she withdraw; and remove from him the responsibility of which he exclaims. Such, his consistency; his disinterestedness; his purity of motive!

As a citizen of a great confederation of Independent States, in some of which slavery exists, the man of Massachusetts, New York, or Illinois, professes to feel that the purity of his political righteousness is stained, because Georgia and Virginia are guilty of the sin, of holding men in slavery. "It can, and must be abolished, and you and I must do it," says Mr. Seward to his Northern hordes. "There is a higher law than the *constitution, which regulates our authority* over the domain."

In like manner, Mr. Sumner, in addressing a New York audience, where there was no negro slavery, thus justifies his attacks upon the institution in other States.

"And now, fellow citizens, what is Slavery? This is no question merely of curiosity or philanthropy, for when the *national Government*, which *you and I at the North help to constitute*, is *degraded to be its instrument*, and all the national territories are proclaimed open to its barbarism, and the constitution itself, is perverted to sanction its pretensions, the whole subject logically and necessarily enters into our political discussion. (Applause). It cannot be avoided, it cannot be blinked out of sight. Nay you must pass *upon it by your votes* at the coming election. *Futile is the plea that we at the North have nothing to do with slavery.*" "Nor can the holy war be ended, until the *barbarism* now dominant in the republic *is overthrown*, and the Pagan power *driven from our Jerusalem.*"

Here he claims the right to overthrow slavery and drive it from the United States, on the ground that the People of "the North helped to constitute the government." Ralph Waldo Emmerson, more than four years ago, proclaimed the incompatibility of the two systems existing together in the same country; and two years before Mr. Lincoln had promulgated it in Illinois and Mr. Seward had re-echoed it in New York, he had announced the "irrepressible conflict"; for which it becomes the South, resolutely to prepare. In a speech delivered at Concord, Mass., in 1856, he thus announces the principle which lies at the foundation of *Political Abolitionism :*

"I do not see how a barbarous community, and a more civilized community can constitute one State. I think we must get *rid of slavery*, or we must get rid of freedom."

In June, 1858, Mr. Lincoln announced the same principle, as follows:

"I believe this government cannot endure permanently, half slave, and half free. Either the *opponents of slavery will arrest* the future spread of it, &c., or its advocates will push it forward, till it shall become alike lawful in all the States."

A few months later in the same year we hear Mr. Seward announcing to his followers the same doctrine :

"Shall I tell you what the collision means? It is an *irrepressible conflict, between opposing* and *enduring forces.* And it means that the United States must and will, sooner or later, become a slave-holding nation, or *entirely a free-labor nation.*"

Such is the foundation principal of the Black Republican platform, as expressed by the New England Poet, the Western Hoosier, and the "New York Politician." It means, when interpreted, that African slavery at the South, because of the Union of the States, is to be warred upon, until it is "utterly extinguished"; and *all* the States become free; for, said Mr. Lincoln in a speech delivered in Chicago 16th July, 1858:

"I have *always hated slavery as much as any abolitionist*. I have always been an old line Whig. I have always *hated* it, and I always believed it in a course of ultimate *extinction*. If I were in Congress, and a vote should come up on a question whether slavery should be prohibited in a new territory, in spite of the Dred Scott decision I would vote that it should."

Now every plea, excuse or palliation which they urge, to justify this "right," which they claim, to meddle with our slave property, and to war on it, to its extinction, is to be found in the fact, That they consider themselves *parts* of the *same nation* with us, and co-actors with us in the *same government*; and that as long as they are so, they are *partakers with us, in the sins* and crimes, and abominations of slavery, such as they are pleased to regard them.

If they were really truthful, and sincere, in this, as their motive, we might respect their conscience, and soon relieve it. "Gentlemen we release you from all your obligations to us, and we withdraw all of ours to you. We dissolve the connection, heretofore existing between us. We have no longer any interest in you; nor you, any in us. Whatever may be our misfortunes, our failings, or our crimes: they are our own; and you are no longer responsible for them. We leave you in peace; not unreasonably expecting the same from you; and that *justice*, simple justice shall mark our intercourse in future."

Would not such a proposition be fair, and meet the approval of every just and Christian man:—that they, who, from a misapprehension of their relative duties to each other, cannot live together as *companions*, without wrangling and hatred, *should separate*, and live, alongside of each other, peaceably, as neighbors. Can any one object to this: especially, when it is considered, that the bond of their companionship, is of such a nature, as to give to each of the parties the undoubted *right* to separate, whenever either of them may judge, for himself, that his happiness requires it?

But will the party, complaining of the offensiveness of our association with them, be *willing* that we should separate from them. Is the pollution of our political morals, which they alledge against us, sufficiently strong to overcome the avaricious longings which they have, for the enormous *pecuniary profits* and *other advantages*, which they derived from their connexion with the *slaveholding* South. I am persuaded not, and that they will cling, fast hold, to us; as long as we shall allow, these conscientious gentlemen, to embrace us. Such is the animating principle of the "irrepressible conflict." The South is to be warred upon until "slavery is extinguished;"—but says Mr. Lincoln, "I do not expect the Union to be *dissolved,*—I do not expect the house to *fall*, but I do expect, it will *cease to be divided;* it will become *all one thing*";—that is, the South *free* by the forcible emancipation of her slaves. Their idea is, to satisfy the *fanatical half* of the Hybrid, by giving up slavery to be extinguished by it; and at the same time, to gratify the *political half* of the ravenous Beast, by keeping the South under its power, ever to be preyed upon—and to minister to its advantage!

Such, fellow citizens of the South, is the scheme of measures which is devised for your destruction:—which it becomes us, to oppose ourselves to, now, and promptly:—else, we shall reap for ourselves hereafter, the contempt of the brave, and leave to our children a heritage of poverty. ●And all this is assumed to be done,—because they say being members of the same Union with them, and subject now to the same government,—they are interested in slavery, and they have a *right* to interfere. How easy then to take away from them this plea. Dissolve the connexion with them and make us *two* people. Stand in the relation to them, of slave-holding Brazil, and slave-holding Cuba; which they do not molest;—because as *foreign* nations, they think, (and think correctly,) that they have no *right* to interfere with their domestic concerns. But, as long as we continue *united* to them as *members* of *the* same *political family*, and as long as we allow them to claim us as "Brethren"; we may expect them to exercise the prerogatives of "Brethren"; and REFORM our morals, according to *their* notions of that sacred relationship, *i. e.*, by exciting our slaves to insurrection; by destroying our property; and burning down our towns, as they are now doing to their "Brethren" in Texas.

G.

Few Southern men appear to be aware, (or if aware, appear disposed, to make proper use) of the immense influence which the Southern (and particularly the "*Cotton States*") exert, over the chief commercial nations of Europe, and especially Great Britain. I make an extract, from a most valuable work, (which I have been so fortunate as to meet with, since the Address was prepared)—entitled, "Southern Wealth and Northern Profits"; which should be in the hands of every Southern man. The author, after a valuable array of Statistics, remarks :

"Of 3,651,000 bales of cotton delivered for consumption in 1859, the United States supplied, 2,880,000 bales, and with these large deliveries, the stock on hand at the close of the year did not increase. Under these circumstances, there is little surprise that the question of cotton supply should become so anxiously discussed, (in Europe). The 'London Cotton Supply Reporter' of Feb'y 3d, remarks:

"Upwards of 500,000 workers are now employed in our cotton factories; and it has been estimated that *at least* 4,000.000 *persons in the country are dependent upon the cotton trade for subsistence*. A century ago Lancashire contained a population of only 300,000 persons; it now numbers 2,300,000. In the same period of time, this enormous increase exceeds that, on any other equal surface of the globe, *and is entirely owing to the development of the cotton trade*. In 1856 there were in the United Kingdom, 2,210 factories, running 28,000,000 spindles, and 209,000 looms, by 97,000 horse power. Since that period, a considerable number of new mills have been erected, and extensive additions have been made to the spinning and weaving machinery of those previously in existence. The amount of actual capital invested in the cotton trade of this kingdom, is estimated to be, between £60,000,000 ($300,000,000) and £70,000,000 sterling ($350,000,000.)

"The quantity of cotton imported into this country in 1859 was 1,181¾ million pounds weight; the value of which at 6d. per lb., is equal to £30,000,000 sterling, (or $150,000,000). Out of 2,829,110 bales of cotton imported into Great Britain, America has supplied us with 2,086,000,—that is 5-7ths of the whole. In other words, out of every 7 lbs. imported from all other countries into Great Britain, America has supplied 5 lbs. India has sent us about 500,000 bales; Egypt about 100,000; South America 124,000, and other countries between 8,000 and 9,000 bales. In 1859, the total value of the *exports* of Great Britain, amounted to £130,513,185; of which £47,020,920, consisted of *cotton* goods and yarns. Thus *more than one-third*, or £1, out of £3. of our entire exports consists of cotton. Add to this, the proportion of cotton, which forms part of £12,000,000 more exported in the shape of mixed woolens, haberdashery, millinery, silks, apparel and stocks. Great Britain alone consumes annually £24,000,000 worth of cotton goods.

"Two conclusions therefore may safely be drawn from the facts and figures now cited ●—first, that the interests of every cotton worker are bound up with *a gigantic trade*, which keeps in motion an *enormous mass of capital*, and this capital, machinery, and labor *depend* for five-sevenths of its employment *upon the Slave States of America for prosperity* and *continuance :*—Secondly that if a *war should at any time break* out between *England and America*, a general insurrection take place among the slaves, disease sweep off the slaves by death, or the *cotton crop should fall short in quantity*, whether from severe frosts, disease of the plants, or other possible causes, *employers would be ruined*, and *famine would stalk abroad among the hundreds and thousands of work people* who are at present fortunately well employed.

" Calculate the consequences for yourself. Imagine a dearth of cotton, and you may picture the horrors of such a *calamity*, from the scenes you may possibly have witnessed when the mills were running only 'short time.' Count np all the *trades*, that are *kept going* out of the wages of the working classes, independent of builders, mechanics, engineers, colliers, &c., employed by the mill owners. *Railways would cease to pay*, and *our ships would lie rotting* in their ports, should a *scarcity of the raw material for manufacture overtake us*."

Such is the *commercial and manufacturing* view of the question, from the leading Journal in Great Britain devoted to those interests more especially. I now give the views of the leading political Journal of that country, to show the influence of cotton on the social and political interests of that mighty nation. I quote again from the work " Southern Wealth and Northern Profits" p. 39.

" The future increase of supply in human clothing, must come altogether from cotton, and every effort to increase the supply, of that article, ends only in a despairing appeal to the United States. The discussion of the question draws that fact; and practical English sense shows itself strongly in the following rebuke, contained in the ' *London Times*,' to Lord Brougham and his confreres:

" 'The import of cotton into this country, has since the import duty was abolished, increased *sixteen* fold. Having been £63,000,000, it is now £1,000,000,000.

" 'This is one of those giant facts, which stand head and shoulders higher than the crowd,—so high and so broad, that we can neither overlook it, nor affect not to see it. It proves the existence of a thousand smaller facts that must stand under its shadow. It tells of sixteen times as many mills; sixteen times as many English families, living by working these mills; sixteen times as much profit, derived from sixteen times as much capital engaged in this manufacture. It carries after it sequences of increased quantity of freights and insurances, and necessities for sixteen times the amount of customers to consume, to profit, the immense amount of produce we are turning out. There are not many such facts as these arising in the quiet routine of industrial history. It is so *large*, and *so steady*, *that we can steer our national policy by it*: it is so apparent to us, that we should be reduced to embarrassment if it were suddenly to disappear. It teaches us to persevere in a policy which has produced so wonderful a result; its *beneficial operation makes it essential to us to deal carefully with it*, now we have got it.' "

" Lord Brougham and the veterans of the old Anti-Slavery Society, do not, we fear, share our delight at this great increase in the employment of our home population. Their minds are still seared by those horrible stories, which were burnt in upon them, in their youth, when England was not only a slave-owning, but even a slave-trading State. Their remorse is so great, that the ghost of a Black man is always before them. They are a benevolent and excellent people; but if a black man happened to have broken his shin, and a White man was in danger of drowning, we much fear that a real anti-slavery zealot, would bind up the black man's leg, before he would draw the white man out of the water. It is not an inconsistency, therefore, that while we see only cause of congratulation in this wonderful increase of trade, Lord Brougham sees in it the exaggeration of an evil he never ceases to deplore. We, and such as we, who are content to look upon society as Providence allows it to exist,—to mend it when we can, but not to distress ourselves immediately, for evils which are not of our creation,—we see only the free and intelligent English families who thrive upon the wages, which these cotton bales produce. Lord Brougham sees only the black laborers who, on the other side of the Atlantic, pick the cotton pods in slavery. Lord Brougham deplores that in this tremendous importation of a thousand millions of pounds of cotton, the lion's share of the profit goes to the United States, and has been produced by slave labor. Instead of 23,000,000, the United States now sends 830,000,000, and this is all cultivated by slaves. There is every reason to believe, that the supply of this *universal necessity* will for many years to come, fail to keep pace with the demand, and in the interest of that large class of our countrymen, *to whom cotton is bread*, we must continue to hope that the United States will be able to supply us in years to come, with twice as much as we bought of them in years past."

H.

It is too great an effort of candor and magnanimity to expect of a Nation, that it will publicly acknowledge a great *political blunder*, by openly retracing its steps. We may therefore not expect that Great Britain will ever attempt to undo the romantic absurdity which she committed, in the emancipation of the slaves in her West India colonies. But, with her present experience, of the utter failure of the whole scheme, and of her great mistake in following the crude theories of her crack-brained fanatics, with even a Lord Brougham at their head;—I think we may safely infer (judging from the tone of her leading journals) that if the act of emancipation was now to be done for the first time, she would most decidedly eschew it. The "*London Times*"—which may be styled the "monarch of the English press"; and exerts a greater sway over British opinion than all the other papers put together, thus alludes to that event.

"There is no blinking the truth. Years of bitter experience—years of hope deferred, of self-devotion unrequited, of poverty, of humiliation, of prayers unanswered, of sufferings derided, of insults unresented, of contumely patiently endured,—have convinced us of the truth. It must be spoken out, loudly and energetically despite the wild mockings of "howling cant." The *freed* West India negro slave *will not till the soil for wages; the free son of the ex-slave* is as obstinate as his sire! He will cultivate lands which he has not bought, for his own yams, mangoes, and plaintains. These satisfy his wants; he does not care for yours. Cotton, and sugar, and coffee, and tobacco—he cares little for them. And what matters it to him, that the Englishman has sunk his thousands and tens of thousands, on mills, machinery, &c., which now totter on the languishing estate, that for years have only returned beggary and debt. He eats his yams, and sniggers at 'Buckra.'

"We know not why this should be; but it is so. The negro has been bought with a price,—the price of English taxation, and English toil. He has been 'redeemed from bondage,' by the sweat and travail of some millions of hard-working Englishmen. Twenty millions of pounds sterling,—one hundred millions of dollars, have been distilled from the brains and muscles of the free English laborer, of every degree, to fashion the West India negro, into a free and independent laborer. 'Free and independent' enough he has become, God knows, but *laborer* he is not; and so far as we can see, he never will be. He will sing psalms and quote texts; but honest, steady industry, he not only detests, but despises!

"We wish to Heaven, that some people in England,—neither government people, nor *parsons*, nor *clergymen*,—but some *just-minded, honest-hearted,* and *clear-sighted* men would go out to some of the Islands,—say Jamaica, Dominica, or Antigua, not for a month, or three months, but for a year, would watch the *precious protege* of English philanthropy,—the '*freed* negro,'—in his daily habits; would watch him as he lazily plants his little *squatting;* would see him, as he proudly rejects agricultural or domestic service, or accepts it only at wages, ludicrously disproportionate to the value of his work. We wish too they would watch him, whilst with a hide thicker than that of a hippopotamus, and a body to which fervid heat is a comfort, rather than an annoyance, he droningly lounges over the prescribed task, on which the intrepid Englishman, uninured to the burning sun, consumes his impatient energy, and too often sacrifices his life. We wish they would go out, and view the negro, in all the blazonry of his idleness, his pride, his ingratitude, contemptuously sneering the industry of that Race, which made him free; and then come home, and teach the memorable lesson of their experience to the *Fanatics*, who have *perverted* him, into *what he is!*"

The contemptuous scorn with which the whole disastrous experiment, together with its *advisers* and *promoters* are here alluded to, indicate the opinions which intelligent Englishmen now entertain on that subject; and how little countenance they would give, towards the emancipation of the Slaves in the Southern States; which would work so much more disastrously, upon all their great interests, than their crazy experiment has done."

I think then that we may confidently expect no hostile intermeddling with our Institution from any of the great powers of Christendom; but on the contrary, if they did not extend to it an active support and protection, seeing that their own prosperity so much depends upon it, that they would at least regard it with the kindliness of friendly neighbors. The only real danger to which it is exposed, arises, 1st from the deadly hostility with which it is pursued by the majority Section of our own country, into whose fatal hands, we, and it, are likely soon to fall; and 2d, from that unaccountable Apathy in the South, which fails to see the approaching danger, and adopt effectual measures for our safety.

I.

It was not convenient, within the limits of an Address, embracing so many topics, to give to this, more than a mere passing notice. But the consequences to the South of having an *Independent* Government of her own, in promoting her public and private wealth, and developing her manufacturing and commercial resources, are such, as to excite the admiration of any one who will carefully examine the subject. Such government will be the basis, and can be the *only* basis of DIRECT TRADE; and the establishment of DOMESTIC MANUFACTURES within her borders. Both depend upon large capital; which can never accumulate at the South, so long as the government, directed by Northern policy, transfers the profits of Southern labor to enrich the North. *Direct trade* enriches all who are engaged in it, populates and builds up cities, multiplies the varieties and numbers of artizans, and trades, and so spreads wealth, and adds to the convenience of the surrounding communities. It is, therefore, the *policy* and *interest* of our cities, and especially of our merchants, to establish Direct trade. But our merchants of the South, (I speak of them as a class), are too feeble, in capital, to contend with the enormous wealth accumulated in the Northern cities, by the policy of the government, to which I have just alluded. Although our merchants have the basis for the most profitable commerce, in the enormous amount of *domestic produce*, furnished by the South, for exportation, they are without the capital (and ever will be whilst in the Union), either to control the shipping necessary to carry it, or to establish those instrumentalities, at home, or abroad, which are necessary to success.

Now the 1st effect of a Southern confederacy, and of having a friendly government will be the abrogation of the present Northern policy, and the substitution of a Southern; which will prevent our wealth from being thus carried away from us.

The 2d effect will be, (by levying duties upon imports, from the North, the same as from the rest of the world), to make it the *interest* of our merchants to 'import direct"—thus avoiding the *double* duties which they would have to pay; first to the Northern confederacy for landing there, and second to the Southern confederacy, where these imports properly belong. *Southern* merchants will then do the business of the South, and our Southern cities reap the richest reward.

From these two consequences of the Southern confederacy, there will spring up a mercantile capital, within a few years, which will be superabundant for all purposes of commerce.

But this will not be all. From this accumulation of capital, and from the wealth and other advantages which Direct Trade will diffuse all around; aided by discriminating duties in favor of articles manufactured within the Southern confederacy. Manufacturing capital will flow in upon us, and all of those Domestic Manufactures *suited to our wants*, will be produced amongst us. What Northern manufacturer, now flourishing under the bounty which he receives from a patronizing Northern policy, amounting to from 20 to 50 per cent., could compete with a Southern manufacturer, within the South; when the circumstances under which the former now comes here, shall be completely reversed : his bounty withdrawn, and transferred to his Southern competitor, who will then wield it against him. If the Shoemakers of Massachusetts, for example, ground down to the point of starvation, by the *Head Shoemakers*, such as Hon. Henry Wilson, the Senator from that State, are compelled to resort to "Strikes" and "Trade Unions" to squeeze out of their masters, a slight additional pittance to eke out their existence, what will be the effect when these bounties are withdrawn, and the profits of these masters diminished or destroyed, by having to meet their Southern competitors having so many advantages in their favour. If they can barely now live, with a large bounty in their favour, how will they fare, when they shall have to *pay out of their profits* the present amount of those bounties in the form of *duties* at the custom houses, before they will be allowed to sell their wares within the territories of the Southern confederacy! In such a case the Shoemakers, and their masters of *Lynn*, and elsewhere must cease to be shoemakers, and take up with another trade; or transfer their capital where they can make it profitable; and what place so suited, as within the bounds of the Southern confederacy, when they will escape the duties at our custom house, and find good customers besides.

The establishment of *Domestic Manufactures* and of *Direct Trade*, with all their immense profits, may then be confidently expected, as the consequences of an independent, and friendly government of our own, whilst it is the most fallacious of all expectations, to look for them under our present circumstances. The exactions made upon us, by the selfish and unequal policy of the North, so long as we continue in the Union, will ever prevent the accumulation of capital at the South, whilst we assist, by our submission to the wrong, to "pile it up" at the North. Since delivering this address, I have seen this subject very forcibly presented by a writer in the city of New York,—" Thomas Prentice Kettel, late editor of the Democratic Review." In his Treatise on "Southern Wealth, and Northern Profits,"* we find these remarks :

" We have followed briefly the progress which each national Section has made in the production of wealth, and have shown that the greatest results, by all odds, have attended the Southern system." " When we turn, however, to *accumulation* and *possession*, a different state of affairs presents itself. Neither the West, nor the South, hold much of what they produce. Wealth once extracted out of the soil by labor, evinces a strong affinity for the North and East; and then piles up, in a magnitude,

---

*This is a work of extraordinary ability; filled with valuable statistics, and important facts; from which the Author makes the most statesmen-like deductions. It should be examined carefully by every Southern man. The unequal operation of the government laws in fostering the interests of one section of the Union, at the expense of the other, is impartially, but forcibly presented; and should nerve the South, to a resolute demand of *all* her rights and a fixed determination, to be satisfied with nothing less.

which dazzles the observer. As the opulent always become *purse-proud*, so does the affluent North regard with a degree of *haughtiness*, the very useful sections, which *pour riches into her lap.* Exercising the prerogative of wealth, she assumes the right to dictate manners, and morality, to those who are less thrifty in worldly matters."

"It is the nature of capital to accumulate, and the more so, when the *laws are framed to favour* that accumulation. From the earliest period of the government the federal revenues have been derived from duties on the goods imported. The duties have not been levied with a *single view to revenue*, but have been so adjusted as to afford the *largest protection* to *Northern manufactures*. In other words, to *tax* the consumers of goods *West* and *South* for the *support* of the *Eastern manufacturers*. The amount of customs so collected, in the last 70 years, reaches *eleven hundred millions* of dollars; a large portion of which was *disbursed at the North!* This sum has been paid mostly by the South and West, into the Federal treasury, on goods imported. The sum of these, may be 20 per cent., of the quantity home manufactured, and the value of which, has been *increased in the ratio of the duty*. If, however it is assumed, that the home-made goods have been enhanced in value, only to the extent of the customs revenue, then the Eastern manufactures have obtained *eleven hundred millions* of *dollars* as *tribute from the South* and *West!!* That large sum has been *taken from agricultural industry* and added to *manufacturing industry.*

"The fisheries of the Eastern States drew $5,000,000, as bounties paid to those engaged in them, out of the federal treasury, to the date of the abolition of those bounties. The *North enjoyed a monopoly* of the *carrying trade;* foreign vessels being excluded. These, and other circumstances, *draw the surplus capital* from the agriculturist, into the *coffers of the manufacturer*. The accumulation of capital thus brought about, became invested in *stocks, Banks, Insurance Companies;* all which drew large profits on *credits granted* to *other sections*. The North has $600,000,000 so invested; of which $356,318,000 are in *banks* alone, which draws $60,000,000, per annum, *from the earnings* of the *other sections*. The frequent pilgrimages from all sections to the Eastern cities, for the purchase of goods, and in pursuit of pleasure, form a large item of cost, charged upon goods, that is paid by the consumer. The profits of other business may be approximated as follows:

Bounties to fisheries per annum,	$ 500,000
Customs, per annum, disbursed at the North,	40,000,000
Profits of manufacturers,	30,000,000
Profits of Importers,	16,000,000
" Shipping imports, and exports,	40,000,000
" on Travelers,	60,000,000
" Teachers and others at the South sent North,	5,000,000
" Agents, Brokers, Commissions, &c.,	10,000,000
Capital drawn from the South,	30,000,000
Total from these sources,	$231,500,000

"This is the approximation of the *annual load which Southern industry is required to carry;* and the means of paying it depends upon *black* labor.

"The *heavy drain of capital* thus created, *prevents* an *accumulation* at the *South* and promotes it as effectually at the *North;* where every such accumulation, only accelerates the drain. If we take the aggregate of these items for ten years only, the result is the enormous sum of $2,315,000,000; and allowing 20 *per cent*. of the sum only, as the aggregate of the 50 years, the amount is 2,770 millions of dollars *earned at the South*, and *added* to *Northern accumulation!!*

"The fishing bounties alone, as we have seen, reach $12,944,000 mostly paid to Maine and Massachusetts. It is not therefore a matter of surprise, if we find the North *very* rich, and the South showing much slower accumulation. No matter how great may be the *production* of wealth at the South, it pours off into the Northern coffers as rapidly as it is accumulated; and, singularly enough, the recipients of that wealth are continually upbraiding the South with its creation. As we have seen, in the quotation from the 'London Times,' contained in a former chapter, English common sense detects the absurdity, not to say the indecency, of such conduct, and is disposed, at least, to be civil, until they can do better."

Now these are startling facts, and should impress themselves deeply on the southern mind. Even if we diminish, or reject altogether, some of the items, as debateable (those for example, of the profits from *Travelers* and *Teachers*) how enormous have been the *pecuniary advantages*, which the North has extracted from the South, by the Union. No wonder then that they should threaten us with fire and sword, if we attempt to leave them. They have no love for us, and we have given them cause, to have no *respect* for us; but they love the "profits" of the connexion: and they intend, if they can, to keep us, as subject colonies, to minister to them, for that purpose. Hundreds of millions of dollars, taken from the agricultural industry of the South, and transferred as a *tribute* through the operation of unjust laws, to the industry of the North! Is any one surprised, that the South thus robbed, is left poor; whilst the North, the robber, overflows with wealth, and "strengtheneth himself in his wickedness." "Thousands of millions,—the lawful earnings of the South, added, during the progress, of the Government, to Northern accumulation"! I ask again, is any one surprised that the North should overflow with capital, to enable her to undertake any, the most gigantic schemes of public improvement, or private enterprise; whilst the South, thus stripped bare of her profits, and left destitute of capital, is unable to build a ship to establish Direct Trade, or to start one enterprise of Domestic manufactures!

Such are the *pecuniary r sults* to the South, of her Union with the North. And when we add to these disastrous results, the contumely, and injustice which we receive, (or which are meditated) at their hands; and find the South willing to submit to these extortions, and continue still united with the men who offer these indignities,—I ask again, should any one be surprised that the North should feel more and more *contempt* for us, and should encroach more and more upon our rights, until, with the incoming of the Black Republican Administration, (which I regard as *certain*) they should drive us to the wall, and spurn us, as the most degraded, and contemptible of dastards! And such will be the verdict of angels, and of men, if the South submit to a rule so detestible, but which, with courage, she can so easily throw off!

www.ingramcontent.com/pod-product-compliance
Lightning Source LLC
Chambersburg PA
CBHW032032090426
42733CB00031B/728